Chronology of Labor in the United States

ALSO BY RUSSELL O. WRIGHT
AND FROM McFARLAND

Chronology of the Stock Market (2002)

*Dominating the Diamond: The 19
Baseball Teams with the Most Dominant
Single Seasons, 1901–2000* (2002)

*A Tale of Two Leagues:
How Baseball Changed as the
Rules, Ball, Franchises, Stadiums and
Players Changed, 1900–1998* (1999)

*Crossing the Plate:
The Upswing in Runs
Scored by Major League Teams,
1993 to 1997* (1998)

*Life and Death in the
United States: Statistics on Life
Expectancies, Diseases and Death Rates
for the Twentieth Century* (1997)

*The Best of Teams, the Worst
of Teams: A Major League Baseball
Statistical Reference, 1903 through 1994* (1995)

*Presidential Elections in the United States:
A Statistical History, 1860–1992* (1995)

*The Evolution of Baseball: A History
of the Major Leagues in Graphs,
1903–1989* (1992)

Chronology of Labor in the United States

RUSSELL O. WRIGHT

McFarland & Company, Inc., Publishers
Jefferson, North Carolina, and London

Library of Congress Cataloguing-in-Publication Data

Wright, Russell O.
    Chronology of labor in the United States / Russell O. Wright.
        p.   cm.
    Includes bibliographical references and index.

    ISBN 0-7864-1444-8 (softcover : 60# alkaline paper)

    1. Labor unions — United States — History — Chronology.
I. Title.
HD6508.W74   2003
331.088'0973'02—dc21   2002151868

British Library cataloguing data are available

©2003 Russell O. Wright. All rights reserved

No part of this book may be reproduced or transmitted in any form or by any means, electronic or mechanical, including photocopying or recording, or by any information storage and retrieval system, without permission in writing from the publisher.

Front cover: Thomas Pollock Anshutz, "The Ironworkers' Noontime," 1880, oil on canvas, 17" × 23⅞" (*Art Today*)

Manufactured in the United States of America

McFarland & Company, Inc., Publishers
  Box 611, Jefferson, North Carolina 28640
        www.mcfarlandpub.com

To Sandra Lynn Wright Carroll Floria

Acknowledgments

I want to acknowledge the huge part my daughter, Terry Ann Wright, played in the preparation of this book. Not only did she do the bulk of the typing of the manuscript itself, she combined the various sections of the book into the formats needed by the publisher.

Terry also created the figures shown in the appendices that bring much more clarity to the text, and she put together much of the index. All of the effort I put into researching the books listed in the bibliography (another section she created) and other sources would have gotten the book no further than the parts of my mind that store new data. She transferred the information from there and turned it into a publishable manuscript.

CONTENTS

Acknowledgments vii
Introduction 1

Chronology of Labor 17

Appendix 1: Percentage of Union Membership in Work Force 1930–2000 109

Appendix 2: Decline in U.S. Farm Workers 1820–1994 113

Appendix 3: Percentage of Women in the U.S. Work Force 1870–2000 115

Appendix 4: Work Stoppages Involving 1,000 Workers or More 1960–2000 119

Appendix 5: Minimum Wage in the United States 1938–2002 121

Appendix 6: Biographies of Key Labor Leaders 123

Bibliography 127

Index 131

INTRODUCTION

This chronology of labor in the United States deals primarily with the history of labor unions and their interactions with the various industries in which the union members were employed. Labor unions did not truly get established until the American Federation of Labor (AFL) was born under Samuel Gompers in 1886 (succeeding the Federation of Organized Trades and Labor Unions that was founded in 1881 with his guiding hand). There were a number of labor organizations formed before the AFL, but the AFL was the first one to hold together for more than just a few years. This chronology will touch on some of these previous organizations (the first truly permanent union was formed in the United States in 1794), but the process of serious labor organization did not begin in the United States until after 1842.

Further, the period of time in which union organizations rose from ineffectuality, to a prominent position in terms of their impact on the labor force; and then fell into a period of decline was surprisingly brief. For example, all labor organizations got a big boost when the New Deal came to Washington with the administration of Franklin Roosevelt in 1933. Legislation was passed that supported the creation of new unions throughout industry, and union membership soared. In 1930, there were only 3.4 million union members, representing only 11.6 percent of the total labor force. By 1945, there were 14.3 union members representing 35.5 percent of the labor force. This was the peak period for unions. After 1945, a year of union arrogance and mismanagement led to the initiation of legislation that was unfavorable for unions, and, by 1965, although union membership was up to 17.3 million, it represented only 28.4 percent of the labor force. Thus, the percentage of the labor force represented by unions dropped 20 percent between 1945 and 1965.

By 2000, union membership had fallen to 16.3 million, representing only 13.5 percent of the labor force, barely more than it was in 1935 at 13.2 percent. The percentage of union representation in the work force fell by 52 percent between 1965 and 2000, and from 1945, it had fallen by 62 percent. It is still falling at that rate. At the biennial convention of the merged AFL-CIO in Las Vegas in December of 2001, President John Sweeny pointed out that in 1955, unions represented one in three workers. At the end of 2001, the ratio was one in eight.

Thus, focusing on the labor union aspect of the chronology of labor means focusing on a 75-year period from 1880 through 1955. There were towering figures in the history of labor unions who operated in that period, and famous (or infamous) events, in terms of the struggle of unions to gain a meaningful foothold in the development of U. S. Industry, took place in that period. Many of those figures and events (which are covered in detail in this chronology) had a substantial impact on the shape of the relationship between employers and employees today. But after 1955, the chronology of labor in the United States was driven by factors other than the growth (and decline) of labor unions. In one sense unions were too successful. Many of the issues they struggled to achieve in the first half of the century are now written into both federal and state law, and the key question about unions today is whether they are still relevant in terms of providing protection for new entrants into the work force that does not already exist in state or federal law.

This chronology also covers (in detail in the Appendices, and at various places in the main body of the book) such items as workforce changes from farming to manufacturing to service occupations, women in the labor force, child labor, the average work week, unemployment compensation, minimum wage, safety in the work place and educational issues. Many new laws upheld by the Supreme Court for the first time came in the revolution in labor laws that took place in the 1930s. Others laws evolved from union contract negotiations beyond the basic questions of higher wages and working conditions on the job. One instance was when Walter Reuther led labor negotiations for the United Auto Workers (UAW) in new directions in the 1940s and 1950s, pursuing "social" issues other than wages and working conditions, and other unions followed his lead. His activities in these areas are covered in detail in this chronology.

A key point in understanding the evolution of labor in the United States is that a "working class" never developed in the United States as it did in Europe. As Daniel Boorstein stated, "We must not look for a class of workers, but for Americans at work." From the earliest days, various labor movements tried to use unions as an instrument for achieving social change but these organizations foundered because they failed to understand that

American workers were not interested in being part of a social experiment. They saw the union only as a vehicle for better wages and working conditions. American workers were mobile to an extent undreamed of in Europe. They could (and did) pack up and head west on a moment's notice, looking for a "better life." They could leave the farm and head for the city (and vice-versa). Organizations such as the Socialists (and later the communists) found that the unions they tried to take over were not interested in "pie in the sky" later; they were interested in better wages and shorter working hours right here and now. This issue of "class" appears again and again in this chronology, and it was a key factor in the demise of several labor organizations, including the Industrial Workers of the World (the IWW) which was born in 1905 and essentially died less than two decades later. Its rise and demise is covered in detail in this chronology.

The course of labor in the United States essentially began in the 1600s with the indentured servants who came from Europe to fill the need for craftsmen and servants alike in the new country. The attraction of this kind of servitude was the fact that wages were much higher in the United States than in Europe. One could work off the terms of indenture (typically seven to fourteen years) and become an established freeman (or woman) in the United States regardless of the level in society in which one existed in the "old country." Artisans also came on their own to bask in the glow of higher incomes in the United States. The British used this process in the early 1700s as a dumping ground for convicted felons. Benjamin Franklin observed that in return the colonies should export their poisonous snakes to England. The Continental Congress passed a resolution that the states should stop accepting "convicted malefactors," but there was money to be made at both ends of the process and the practice died out slowly. Other types of indentured service began to be cut back in England in the 1700s because of a concern that England would run short of labor itself.

A new source of labor developed when the British indentured servant approach began to fade in Britain. Poor peasants in various Western Europe countries started to sign up after arriving in America as "redemptioners." Their price in terms of the number of years of servitude required to gain their freedom was dependent on the market conditions existing when they arrived in the States. Their price depended also on their skills and the cost of their transportation that had to be repaid. These peasants often came as entire families, and were thus more acceptable in the colonies than convicted felons. The work was often hard and conditions unpleasant, but it was estimated that more than half of the indentured labor that came to the States before the Revolutionary War was made up of these peasant groups.

The attraction to these groups was that there were many (true) stories about peasants, who were at the lowest level of society in their own country, becoming landowners themselves in the new country. This was essentially the beginning of the surge of immigrants who would come to the states in the decades ahead, filling what would be the fourth largest nation in the world in terms of square miles. Many would become farmers to realize their dream of being landowners, and, showing the mobility of the American work force, would return to the manufacturing and service sectors when the development of farm mechanization reduced the need for farmers. For example, in 1820, 71.8 percent of the workforce in the United States was employed in farm occupations. The population of the United States in 1820 was 9.6 million. By 1960, when the population was 179.3 million (almost 20 times as much as in 1820), only 6.1 percent of the population was engaged in farming occupations. As the population grew by 20 times, the percentage of the work force necessary to supply them with food fell by a factor of 12. This huge shift from a country of farmers to a country of manufacturing and service occupations is also discussed as part of this chronology.

As the United States grew and prospered in the 1600s, regulations concerning the labor force grew as well. In 1621, wage scales began to be established in Virginia, and in the early 1630s wage scales were set in Massachusetts. These early steps in the regulation of labor led to the inevitable development of guilds, trade groups, and unions. By 1648, guilds had been formed in Boston for Coopers and Shoemakers. There was also a rebellion among indentured servants in Virginia in 1676. But very little organized action took place on either side until the late 1700s. The United States was still a country of farmers, and the "Plantation System" in the south depended on the slave trade (in essence indentured servants whose period of indenture was forever) to keep producing tobacco and cotton. The Revolutionary War in 1776 and the following war of 1812 proved to be a big help to manufacturing in the States. With England cut off or definitely non-preferred as a supplier, demands were high in the states for replacement goods, even though many people felt it was not desirable to have the United States join the industrial revolution. They felt it was "better" to keep the agricultural system that most people (about 90 percent of the work force) were engaged in at the time. Even a famous person such as Alexander Hamilton had to plead for an emphasis on new manufacturing efforts, but many people felt the United States could not compete with Britain in the marketplace.

Eli Whitney played a big part in helping to develop a manufacturing sector in the States. He invented the cotton gin in 1793 to separate the fiber of short–staple cotton from the seed, and although people who copied his gin in spite of his patent kept him from making big money from his invention, textile factories sprung up in New England (most employing women and children at low wages). Samuel Slater, a young Englishman who came to the States about the same time had committed to memory the textile machinery with which he worked in England (its export was forbidden), and started cotton mills in Rhode Island for his employers, who had hired him for this purpose. Other mills were built in New England, but many failed due to severe competition from the more experienced British.

However, the Napoleonic Wars, which gave rise to the Embargo Act enacted by the U.S. Congress in 1807, and the subsequent war of 1812 with the British had the effect of restricting trade with England. Prices of imported cotton rose, and capital flowed into the textile industry. The number of cotton spindles in the United States rose from 8,000 in 1807 to 130,000 in 1815. Ironically, Whitney's invention of the cotton gin, by providing a means of profitably expanding the plantation system in the south, gave a new push to the need for slaves. Although the slave trade terminated in 1808, at which time there were estimated to be less than one million slaves in the States (compared to a total population of about 7.2 million in 1810), the demand for cotton created a higher price for slaves, encouraging planters to support the addition to the slave population by natural increase and some illegal importation. By 1860, just before the Civil War, it was estimated there were a total of 4 million slaves (compared to a total population of 31.4 million). After the Civil War, these slaves would become part of the work force, and would make many "northern" unions face up to the fact that they were as discriminatory toward blacks as any "southern" union.

Whitney made an additional contribution to the manufacturing sector by developing the technique of standardized, interchangeable parts. He built a firearms factory near New Haven in 1798 that produced muskets made with this approach, thus essentially creating modern mass production. By 1850, this technique was being used to manufacture clocks, watches, locks, agricultural implements and sewing machines. At the International Exhibition of 1851 in London, many European technical experts realized that factories in the United States were building cheaper, mass produced goods that exceeded the European goods in quality. And, as noted before, at this time only about 10 percent of the labor force in the United States was involved in this kind of manufacturing effort. The rest were still farming.

It was against this background that labor unions slowly evolved in the early 1800s in the United States. Most unions were created to solve just one issue (usually wages and/or working hours). Once the issue was resolved one way or another, the union disbanded. The first union is generally agreed to be a society of Philadelphia Shoemakers in 1792. It was replaced by The Federal Society of Cordwainers (Shoemakers) in 1794, also a group assembled by the 1792 Philadelphia Shoemakers. This 1794 union is sometimes acknowledged as the first "permanent" union, although it ended in 1806 after losing a court case where it was found guilty of criminal conspiracy for founding a union and striking.

This fate was shared by many would-be unions. It was considered illegal to even join a union because unions "conspired" to raise wages. But a decision by the Massachusetts Supreme Court in 1842 addressing a case brought against (once again) some journeymen shoemakers in 1840 reversed their conviction for "improper conduct" for being members of a union. Chief Justice Lemuel Shaw, a widely respected judge, ruled that simply joining a union was not a criminal act. After all, the union might well come together for a beneficial purpose. It would have to be proved that the union actually committed an act of "oppression and injustice" before an injunction could be sought against it. Shaw's ruling was actually effective only in Massachusetts, but the high regard in which he was held resulted in his decision becoming effective beyond the borders of Massachusetts. The decision became a charter and a landmark for the formation of new unions. The timing was just right, because the financial panic of 1837 had caused a depression that essentially wiped out all unions formed prior to then. The depression was ending just as the new ruling came down from Judge Shaw. As a result, Union activity grew rapidly in the 1840s.

In the United States in the following years there were some issues of law that had much to do with labor in general and unions specifically and that still affect our lives today. Much of our history in all aspects has been played out in the courts, and with the propensity of Americans to sue each other at a moment's notice for real or perceived wrongs, this condition will almost certainly exist far into the future. An excellent summary of these legal issues is provided in *An Introduction to Labor Law* by Michael Evan Gold, a slim volume containing much useful knowledge, and upon which key information in this text is based.

First, it is necessary to change our perception of who writes the laws in the United States. It is not the legislatures of the states or our Congress. It is somewhat true that legislatures write the law and courts interpret it and apply it. But in the recent past, in the days of Judge Shaw, for example, the courts essentially made the laws up as they went. There were relatively few statutes passed by legislatures, and judges ruled as they felt individually guided by custom and decisions that had built up over centuries of doing business. This body of knowledge was known as the "common law." This is a direct inheritance from England, and the common law still affects our lives today, although much less than it used to. Judge Shaw actually wrote a new law with his interpretation of the common law as he saw it when he applied it to the question of unions.

Courts continue to make our laws today even when the number of statutes written by legislatures seems literally endless. If the case of A vs. B falls exactly within the statute, we can say that the legislature has written the law that governs the case. But if the case of C vs. D varies slightly from what is outlined in the statute, the judge handling the case essentially writes a new law when he decides if the statute applies to the new case, and, if so, who has the winning position. This new law will be used as a precedent for subsequent cases of the C vs. D type. Precedent is extremely important, because by knowing that judges give it great weight, people planning business decisions have a basis for knowing what the legalities of their new decision will likely be. Precedent is not just an easy way out for the next ruling judge; it prevents chaos in that it keeps a body of law up to date. The first judge to rule on C vs. D cases thus writes the law for all new cases of that type. Now we come to E vs. F that differs slightly from all prior cases. Another judge writes another new law, and so on and so forth. The original statute can be obsolete in practice, but a new body of law has evolved, all written by the courts. Anyone familiar with the incredibly complex Tax Code used by the IRS knows that the process I have just described has produced much of that code.

In this way the courts, in times when unions were in disfavor because of the tactics they used to pressure employers to yield to their demands, would write laws that gave employers (business) ways to curtail union activities (even when unions were very much in favor in the depression and legislators were passionately writing laws to help them, the key issue was which statute would and which would not be approved by the Supreme Court—many were not). But the normal court process of presenting evidence to convince a jury could be very tedious and slow. When juries consisted mainly of shopkeepers and landowners, businesses were agreeable to "taking their chances" of an agreeable and quick verdict with minimal evidence. By the end of the nineteenth century, when all men could vote and thus workers began to show up more often on juries, the potential slowness of the legal process without the assurance of a favorable verdict became intolerable to business (if your company had been forced into bankruptcy by an ongoing strike or boycott, finding that in the end your cause was just brought very little satisfaction).

Employers decided to take their cases to the civil courts, because there they found a perfect weapon. It was the injunction. An injunction is an order from a court requiring a person either to do or stop doing specific acts. A person can be sent to jail for violating an injunction. An injunction can be obtained in as little as one day, and an injunction is issued by a judge, not a jury. Find an agreeable judge, and you can stop the union from picketing that same day, and the order has teeth with the threat of jail time. This is why injunctions became the great enemy of unions.

A related legal issue that must be covered to help fill in the background against which organized labor developed in the United States is the question of antitrust laws. In 1890, Congress passed the Sherman Antitrust Act to control monopolies in business. This act was specifically aimed at the great oil trust developed by the original John D. Rockefeller. It did eventually break up the trust, but most people don't remember that in Rockefeller's heyday the prime use of oil was to generate kerosene for the lamps of the world. When the growth of the automotive business in the 1900s created a huge demand for gasoline, the companies that remained after the breakup of Rockefeller's trust became more powerful and profitable than Rockefeller ever considered in his wildest dreams of empire.

As far as unions were concerned, the Sherman Act had another great defect. It cast its net so widely that it could be applied to Labor Unions as well. The statute outlawed "every combination ... or conspiracy in restraint of trade or commerce among the several states." Samuel Gompers, founder of the AFL, shuddered at the familiar word "conspiracy" and gloomily predicted that the Sherman Act, felt by most to be a help or at least neutral towards labor, would eventually be used against labor. He was absolutely correct, as is detailed in the chronology section of the book.

Further emphasizing the role that the courts play in writing the laws we live under, after much effort by Gompers and others, the Clayton Act was passed in 1914 to specifically exempt unions from the effects of the Sherman Act. Union leaders, including Gompers, hailed the Clayton Act as the "Magna Carta of Labor." However, after World War I, the good feelings towards unions engendered by their restraint of strikes (except for the ill-fated IWW) to keep goods flowing for the war effort came to an end. With a new atmosphere in the air, companies attacked the poorly written Clayton Act on grounds that the courts upheld, and injunctions were flying everywhere. So much for Labor's Magna Carta. That had to wait until the depression.

All of this was far into the future when Judge Shaw gave new life to labor with his 1842 ruling. Union activity grew rapidly in the 1840s, and by 1852 a National Typographical Union was formed which is generally recognized as the first national union to remain in permanent existence.

Samuel Gompers was born in 1850 in London, and his emigration to the United States in 1863 marked the beginning of a truly organized labor movement in the United States (culminating in the birth of the AFL in 1886). The period of growth following Judge Shaw's verdict marks the beginning of the detailed chronology section that follows this introduction. In this period the population of the country grew from 23.2 million in 1850 to 123.2 million by 1920, an increase of exactly 100 million. The increase alone was bigger than the total population of most other countries. The United States became the manufacturing and financial colossus of the world after World War I left much of Western Europe in financial, if not physical, ruin. The interplay between labor and management from the late 1840s onward included many bloody strikes and legal victories and defeats on both sides as outlined in this introduction and detailed in the chronology.

As the 1920s got underway, unions were on the defensive. Many people had been soured by the actions of the Industrial Workers of the World (the IWW) during the war. The IWW (informally known as the "Wobblies") was born in 1905. They are one of the most romanticized movements of the 1900s, but they never had a chance of succeeding with their woolly-headed philosophy. The first sentence of the preamble to their constitution stated that "the working class" and the "employing class" have nothing in common. The sense of class warfare pervaded the entire organization and its functioning. The IWW was going to build one big union that would include every worker in the United States. Then they would call one big strike that would bring the country to its knees. This would force the powers that be to turn everything over to the workers who would build heaven on earth. Their cherished leader, "Big Bill" Heywood, took the sense of class to an extreme when he declared that "it is better to be a traitor to your country than to your class." This ultimately led to the destruction of the union after World War I on the basis that it was a treasonous organization.

Further, the association of unions with socialism, communism, and other "radical" movements in the minds of many others did not help. Strikes had reached a peak of 4,450 in 1917, before the United States entered World War I in 1918 (the huge number of strikes in 1917 would not be exceeded until 1937), but the number of workers affected by strikes in 1919 was three and one-half times the number affected in 1917. Unions were held in low regard, and they struggled throughout the decade of the 1920s.

Everything changed in the 1930s. The much publicized "crash" of the stock market in the fall of 1929 put much of the business industry on alert that bad days might be coming, following a decade of growth in the 1920s. Actually, the stock market recovered quite nicely by the spring of 1930. On April 17, 1930, the market was only four percent below its closing value of "Black Thursday" on October 24, 1929, just six months earlier. Government officials with the Hoover administration (including the President himself) were telling everyone that the depression was over. The best date one could pick for the beginning of the depression was April 17, 1930. In the next two years the stock market fell another 66 percent, reaching a low in July of 1932. It would be 1954 before the market regained its highs of 1929. By the time Franklin Roosevelt took office in March of 1933, a depression was underway in which as many as 13 million would be claimed to be unemployed at some point, and the unemployment rate would be claimed to have reached 25 percent. Acting on the impulse that said whatever we had been doing wasn't working and that was time to try something—almost anything—new, the Roosevelt Administration started Congress writing new legislation to correct past sins. The ways financial markets operated (including banks and the stock market) were changed substantially, and it was concluded that the

Introduction

plight of workers would be greatly improved if unions had the legal ability to organize them and then serve as their negotiating agent with private businesses. A true Magna Carta of Labor was about to appear. It probably will be no surprise to learn that just as unions were about to win their greatest victory, they started fighting among themselves. It certainly was not the first time in history that, when it became clear that there were going to be some spoils to divide, the long suffering groups who were going to get them started battling over who was going to get the biggest piece.

To understand what the battle was about, although it is covered in detail in the chronology that follows, some union terminology needs to be introduced. The AFL based its organization on assembling what are known as "craft" or "trade" unions (the AFL was not a union, per se. It was an umbrella organization with which other unions were "affiliated," and organizing benefits and money flowed from individual unions to the umbrella and back again). In trade unions, all union members practice the same trade (such as making tools) no matter where they are employed. They were organized "horizontally" if you will. In this way they were an "elite" organization. Each member was a well-trained specialist with hard-to-replace skills. They were relatively well paid, generally spoke English, and absolutely white. There were no blacks (or shades of almost any hue other than white), and women were rare. When the AFL conducted organizing drives, they had no interest in the many immigrants and minorities doing mass production work where often the only "skill" needed was turning a machine off and on.

As President of the AFL, Samuel Gompers sincerely believed that his methods of organizing the workforce were the only ones that would work, and, indeed he succeeded in keeping the AFL alive for 38 years while many other contenders had failed. Gompers was the key spokesman for labor when the Wilson administration was in Washington from 1912 through 1920, and he played a big role in getting the Clayton Antitrust bill enacted in 1914. But many objective people, including his supporters, agreed that he was in many ways a bigot. Gompers died in 1924, and his successor, William Green, continued his basic policies.

Within the AFL organizers led by John L. Lewis, who would become infamous for his arrogant battles with the government in the 1940s as head of the coal miners union, had been trying to develop what would come to be called "industrial" unionism. In this approach, all the workers in one industry would be part of one union, regardless of their specific jobs. They would organize "vertically." It was felt this approach would work better in the emerging mass production industries, such as automobile manufacturing, which had become the largest single manufacturing industry in the United States, employing half a million workers, by 1929. The group under Lewis, supported strongly by Philip Murray, started as the Committee for

Industrial Organization (CIO), and started organizing in 1935, the same year the Wagner Act, Labor's true Magna Carta was enacted. The CIO was expelled from the AFL in 1937, and 1938 it set up shop as a truly independent organization, changing its name to the Congress for Industrial Organization, but generally being known as simply the CIO. It was immensely successful, and in 1955 the two groups merged as the AFL-CIO, and they have remained together since. At the time of the merger, the long-established AFL claimed about 10 million members, while the brash new CIO claimed about 5 million.

While the union infighting, described in detail in the following chronology, was going on, the Roosevelt administration was giving labor everything it wanted. The Wager Act of 1935 was the key, and when it was upheld as constitutional in 1937, labor unions grew astronomically. Even today, some union old-timers look back on the upheavals of the 1930s as the "good old days." Many individuals suffered severely in the depression, but it was a time when unions were finally given all the big guns they needed, and they turned them on "business" with glee. The unions also had the benefit of good timing in that they established themselves firmly in the labor force just as World War II lifted the United States out of its long depression. The unions agreed to a no-strike pledge after Pearl Harbor, but it was a pledge more "honored in the breach than in the observance." However, government money was pouring into all sectors of the economy and the National War Labor Board kept cost-of-living increases flowing. Money was everywhere. The unions and their members prospered during the war years. But their generally arrogant behavior would come back to haunt them after the war.

It is no exaggeration to say that in just a little over one year, from the formal surrender of Japan on September 2, 1945, to the Congressional elections in early November of 1946, the unions trashed all of the good relations they had enjoyed with the American people since the depression began in the early 1930s. What's more, in this period, it can be said that the unions started the continual decline they suffered during the rest of the century as outlined at the beginning of this Introduction. Strikes rained down on the American people in 1945 and 1946 just as allied bombs had rained down on the Axis during the war. The unions seemed determined to prove the accuracy of Lord Acton's statement that "Power tends to corrupt; absolute power corrupts absolutely." If something was not going to be done the union way, it was not going to be done at all. As discussed in detail in the chronology, the worst offender, both during and after the war, was John L. Lewis and his coal miners.

Based on his actions after 1940, a serious question could be raised as to whether Lewis was suffering from initial signs of senility. He was 60 years old in 1940 when he said he would resign from the Presidency of his beloved

CIO if Roosevelt were re-elected in 1940 (the two men, once friends, had been driven apart by Lewis' irrational actions as described in the chronology). Then Lewis did resign following Roosevelt's election to the once unthinkable third term (Lewis took it as a vote of non-confidence in him by Labor). In 1942 he took his United Mine Workers union out of the CIO, and embarked on what seemed to be a one-man effort to destroy the good relationship with the public the unions had developed by the end of the depression. And he succeeded.

Lewis was the son of a Welsh coal miner, and Lewis himself had started working in the mines as a young man. He worked up through the ranks step-by-step to become President of the United Mine Workers in 1920. Then he built the CIO in the next 18 years in the same way. However, in spite of his successes, Lewis had become one of the most dangerous kinds of men. He "knew better." The only voice he would listen to was his own. And his final course of action was to cause the destruction of what he had helped build.

There was a serious warning sign in 1943 when the Smith-Connally bill was enacted over Roosevelt's veto on June 25, 1943, two days after Lewis called the coal miners out on strike for the second time in two months, in spite of the no strike pledge during the war. It was the first anti-labor bill to pass Congress in a generation, and it was passed by a Democratic Congress over the veto of a Democratic President (who had, in essence, been supporting the antics of Lewis by insisting that, as President, he preferred voluntary compliance than strict legislation). Many had had their fill of Lewis and his arrogance.

But Lewis took no notice. One of the worst strikes in the period after the war came when Lewis took his coal miners out again and again as he disputed settlements he had previously agreed to (the miners were always anxious to do his bidding because he nearly always got them increased income and benefits). This time President Truman took Lewis to court, and Lewis was finally found in contempt and personally fined $10,000 and the union $3.5 million. The Supreme Court upheld the fine, but reduced it to $700,000 on the basis that Lewis must comply with the strike settlement or the fine would go back to $3.5 million. Lewis complied.

There are more details of this and the other strikes in this period (unions in other industries often took their cue from Lewis because he always seemed to come out ahead) in the chronologies, but Lewis and his copycats had overplayed their hands this time. The public had had enough of unions and their strikes. Nearly every union member ultimately got an increase of 18.5 cents per hour to make up for what the unions claimed they had lost during the war. But the public then blamed the unions for the surge of inflation after the war. In the Congressional Elections of 1946, a conservative Congress was elected with, as they saw it, a mandate to curb the power of unions. They responded with the Taft-Hartley bill, which President Truman vetoed on June 20, 1947. Congress easily and quickly overrode the veto. Thus, a "super majority" was required in Congress to pass the bill, which shows the degree of support it had. The house overrode the veto by 311 to 83, and the Senate did so by 68 to 25 with 2 not voting. Labor responded by calling it a "slave labor" act and made its repeal their prime political objective. This "my or no way" approach, which was a carry over from their depression gains, killed any chance the unions had of modifying the bill. Taft was willing to make changes after the famous election of 1948, in which President Truman scored a big upset, but the unions wanted repeal or nothing. They got nothing, and, in essence, an ongoing decline ever after.

Another issue related to unions and the courts needs to be defined to help understand some of the things that happened after the Wagner Act was passed in 1935, and certified by the Supreme Court in 1937. The term "labor law" is actually very narrow. It applies only to laws covering the relationships between unions and private employers. The primary laws involved in this arena are the Norris-LaGuardia Act of 1932, the Wager Act of 1935, the Taft-Hartley Act of 1947, which revised the Wagner Act, and the Landrum Griffith Act of 1959, which further modified the Wagner Act. This body of law does not cover Public Employers such as federal, state and local governments, and it does not cover employees of railroads or airlines, or agricultural workers and independent contractors. In addition, since the Wagner Act came into being in 1935, a number of new laws have been written to cover such things as minimum wages, health and safety on the job, unemployment insurance, pension plans, race and sex discrimination, and so forth. This body of law has come to be called "employment laws." But "labor law" relates only to the dealings between unions and private employers. Other laws generally have been written to cover the categories of workers exempted above. With courts "writing" new laws every day as described before, it is easy to see that the complexity of laws dealing with issues related to the work force have grown beyond belief, and possibly beyond rational management. It is also possible to see one reason why unions have been on the decline since the 1940s. If so many other laws exist to "protect" the functioning of the work place, what do unions now bring to the party?

The unions were wrapped up in the issue of communists in the labor movement as 1950 approached, and a number of unions, especially in the CIO, were expelled for communist activity. In 1952, President Philip Murray of the CIO died at the age of 66 on November 9, and President William Green of the AFL died just 12 days later on November 21 at the age of 79. Ironically, both men started out in the United Mine Workers Union and had been close friends of John L. Lewis, and each other at one time. Lewis was 72 in 1952 and still active. The question of an AFL-CIO merger had come up once more, and the long-time presidents of the two organizations, Murray and Green, were actually the key stumbling block, because neither wanted to bring his organization under the direction of the other.

George Meany, previously the secretary-treasurer of the AFL, became the new President of the AFL, and Walter Reuther, President of the United Automobile Workers, became the new President of the CIO. Both were in favor of a merger, and after much negotiating, the merger of the AFL-CIO became official in 1955 with George Meany as the President of the combined organization. The combined organization had over 15 million members in 1955, which made it the largest union organization in the history of the United States, and, for that matter, the free world. At the time, total union membership in the United States was 16.8 million, representing 33.2 percent of the labor force. The merged organization has held together ever since, even though its influence has fallen steadily as measured as a percentage of the labor force.

The next seminal event in the interaction of the labor force and employers in the United States occurred in May of 1970 when Walter Reuther was killed in the crash of a private jet that was trying to land at a Family Education Center the United Automobile Workers (UAW) was building for its members in Northern Michigan. Reuther was a towering figure in the labor movement. He was elected President of the UAW in 1946, and was a fundamental supporter of the CIO in its early days. He was elected President of the CIO in 1952 and guided its merger with AFL in 1955. But just as John L. Lewis and Philip Murray had done before him, Reuther kept the Presidency of his own union (the UAW) and treated the Presidency of the CIO as a part-time job. He was more than happy not to contest George Meany for the job of President of the combined AFL-CIO.

Reuther was a socialist at heart, just as his father Valentine had taught him in family discussions around the dinner table. The three younger Reuther boys (Walter, Roy, and Victor) learned at the knee of their father, and all three made careers in some way involved in unions. After becoming President of the UAW, Walter Reuther led some legendary negotiating efforts with General Motors, initiating the concept of long-term contracts in an effort to gain many union benefits in terms of pensions, cost-of-living adjustments (COLA), and profit sharing that were beyond the usual issues of wages and working conditions in the factories. These efforts are described in detail in the chronology that follows.

Reuther pulled the UAW out of the AFL-CIO in 1968 in what was really a personal dispute with George Meany, but this time no other unions followed Reuther's lead into uncharted waters. The UAW eventually returned to the fold after Reuther's death, but no one could replace Reuther's unique ability to find new places for unions to go and to take the initiative in leading them there. When John L. Lewis died in relative obscurity at the age of

89 in 1969, and then Meany himself died in 1980, still in the saddle at the age of 86, the labor leaders who were essentially responsible for the rise of labor in the 1900s were gone.

Meany was replaced by his executive assistant, (Joseph) Lane Kirkland, but Kirkland could not stop the decline of unions. He was effectively forced to resign in August of 1995, and was replaced by "young Turk" John Sweeny in the first contested election in AFL-CIO history later in 1995. The decline may have slowed by 2001, but the answer to the question of whether unions are still relevant today is the subject of much controversy and essays and agonizing within the AFL-CIO itself. Stated as simply as possible, much of what unions offered to their followers in the past is now provided by federal and state laws covering activities in the workplace. The prime constituency of the union historically, the so-called blue collar worker, now makes up less than 25 percent of the workforce, even if it is counted in the most favorable "blue collar" way. Unions, once strongly opposed to illegal immigration because it was seen as competition for union jobs, now embrace illegal immigration as a potential source of new union members. The steps unions are taking to once again become "relevant" are described in detail in the chronology that follows. But plans are comparatively easy to make. Finding new leaders who can implement them is much harder. New versions of John L. Lewis and Walter Reuther are not presently in sight. And the decline of unions in the private sector seems likely to go on indefinitely.

Chronology of Labor

As discussed in the Introduction, labor in the sense of organized labor did not become a reality in the United States until a ruling by the Massachusetts Supreme Court in 1842 essentially made it legal to form labor unions. Thus, this chronology begins after that ruling was handed down. It is highly recommended that the Introduction be read first, both to have an understanding of the flow of the book, and also to learn about how labor (and manufacturing) developed in the United States before 1842, even if all attempts at organizing labor before 1842 failed to succeed for more than just a few years. The first national union considered to remain in permanent existence was the International Typographical Union, which was formed in 1852 following a series of meetings that began in 1850 and with which we begin our chronology.

December 2, 1850—A convention began in New York with the objective of forming some sort of national association for the various typographical groups that had been building in various cities during the 1840s. The New York association took the lead in calling for the convention, and groups in Boston and Philadelphia quickly agreed. The convention finally had delegates from six different cities, and groups from five other cities sent "communications" to the meeting. A theme of the convention that would be duplicated over and over in future years in other conventions was a call for the formation of local unions everywhere. A national executive committee was formed, a second convention was held in Baltimore in September of 1851, and by 1852 the International Typographical Union had been established on a national basis.

July 5, 1859—A convention was held in Philadelphia on this date to form a national union for the Iron Molders. Once again there had been a number of local organizations that had been operating since the 1840s which had sporadically tried to form a national association, but they did not succeed until now. A notable event in the formation of the Iron Molders Union was that William H. Sylvis, who had been Secretary of the Philadelphia local, failed in his run for President of the national union but was elected national treasurer.

Sylvis would become a national figure in union organizing in the future. He believed that cooperation with employers was the best way to achieve the goals of labor. When the union suffered significant defeats in 1867 and 1868, he was among the first to become disillusioned with the strike as a weapon. Eugene V. Debs, who ultimately ran for President of the United States on the Socialist ticket, said he drew on the views of Sylvis in formatting his personal view of Labor relations.

January 28, 1861—The Union of American Miners was organized in West Belleview, Illinois. This particular version of a miner's union would last only to the end of the decade due to much internal dissension, but the issue of a miner's union would continually reappear in future years. Finally, the organization that was formed in 1888–1890 would become one of the great driving forces for labor thereafter, especially after it fell under John L. Lewis in 1920.

January 1, 1863—This was the date President Lincoln's famous Emancipation Proclamation became effective. It was in many ways largely a symbolic act, but it can be counted as the first step in a process that would add an appropriation proportion of the estimated four million slaves to the nation's workforce when the Civil War ended. In this way it can also be counted as the first step in the great migration of blacks from the South to the rest of the country, most notably initially to the North and the Midwest, and, after World War II, to the far west.

May 8, 1863—The first union to be organized on the railroads, the Brotherhood of Locomotive Engineers, was formally organized on this date. It had existed since the 1850s, although some say it originated even earlier, and the name "brotherhood" was deliberately chosen to avoid the word "union." Either way, the union founded on this date has been one of the most stable labor unions in American labor history (it adopted its exact present name in 1864). The railroads in the 1800s were the biggest single driver of economic growth in the United States, and the first union in this area of the economy was a significant event.

July 29, 1863—Samuel Gompers, then 13, arrived in New York with his family after a 50-day voyage from London. Thirteen years later Gompers would become President of the American Federation of Labor, a position he would hold until his death in 1924. Gompers would become a leading figure for organized labor, and is the first of the "Big Six" American Labor Leaders summarized in Appendix 6.

Samuel Gompers, and his father, Solomon, were cigar makers by trade in London. Samuel had fond memories of his life as a child laborer. Cigar rolling was a very quiet business, so much so that one of the men would be assigned as a reader. The other men would share their output with him so that the reader would suffer no loss of income. The reader's job was to search out articles of interest in the local newspapers and magazines, cutting a wide swath in terms of culture, politics, and economics. His job was to pique the interest of his listeners so that all could share in the lively discussions that followed his readings.

The cigar makers acted as a mutual aid society, and among other things, they created an emigration fund for those who wanted to go to the United States. This is how the Gompers family managed to finance their passage to New York in 1863. In the usual fashion of the times, Solomon Gompers followed his brother-in-law and many old friends to the States, and he in turn was followed by at least two dozen cousins, nearly all of whom were cigar makers. With the help of all these relatives, the Gompers family quickly found a four-room apartment in a Houston Street tenement, and immediately began rolling cigars at home.

February 13, 1865—On this date the iron and steel workers agreed to a plan that would set the level of their wages in proportion to the price the manufacturers received for the product (iron). It was the first time that this arrangement (otherwise known as a sliding scale of wages) was used in the United States. The Civil War had increased demand for the products of iron mills, and this was a favorable time for wage increases. The sliding scale approach was looked upon favorably by each side because it reduced the need for frequent meetings to adjust the wage rate, and in a time of rising prices the unions were happy to endorse such a system.

August 20, 1866—A convention was held in Baltimore to form a national labor federation. Its principal goal would be the establishment of the 8-hour day using the power of an affiliation of individual national unions. William Sylvis, of the Iron Molders Union, was asked to draw up a proposed constitution for the new organization, which would be called the National Labor Union. His constitution was adopted in 1867. Sylvis pressed for cooperation with employers and also called out for political action in an attempt to get labor to try to get political help to achieve its aspirations.

Sylvis died suddenly at the age of 41 in 1869, and, after his death, the National Labor Union soon fell apart. It evolved essentially into a political organization, and it disappeared after its candidate for President in the 1872 election, Judge David Davis of Illinois, withdrew when he failed to get the Democratic nomination.

April 6, 1868—A group called the Workingmens Benevolent Association was chartered by the Court of Common Pleas of Schuylkill County in the Pennsylvania coalfields northwest of Philadelphia. The key leader was John Siney, who started work at the age of seven in the coalmines in England after his family was evicted from his native Ireland. After immigrating to the States in 1863, Siney was hired by the Benevolent Association and ultimately became its leader. Just days after the group was chartered, the Governor of Pennsylvania signed an eight-hour mining law on April 14, an outgrowth of the fact that the Congress passed legislation in 1868 enabling an 8-hour day for Federal employees. As was common in those days, passing legislation was one thing, having it enforced was another.

The Pennsylvania coal-mining operators immediately agreed to the 8-hour day, but insisted on a wage cut to compensate for the lost hours. The miners struck, and the mine operators waited for the then high coal stocks to be drawn down. In a month the coal piles were sufficiently lowered, and the operators ended the strike by offering a ten percent wage increase. The strike had the effect of greatly increasing the power of the Benevolent Association, which had conducted the negotiations. When similar strikes followed, a sliding scale arrangement was negotiated that tied wages to the prices paid for coal at Port Carbon and Elizabeth, the key shipping points for coal mined in Schuylkill County. This arrangement went on until 1875, when the unions were finally broken by a six-month strike that they ultimately lost. It would be another quarter century before effective unions would appear again in the anthracite coalfields. A prime result of this vacuum was the growth both in influence and violence of the "Molly Maguires," a murderous "secret society" formed at a time when such societies suddenly came into vogue, partly to avoid being stuck with the word "union," which generally still carried a negative connotation. The Molly Maguires began in the early 1840s, and to some extent, they were the only game in town when the Workingmens Benevolent Association ceased to exist. A series of murders followed that were not so much based on strikes and labor negotiations but on the desire for revenge of real or imagined slights against certain coal operators, hated supervisors, and even other members of the secret society. The Molly Maguires were in no way a union organization, but rather a nasty instrument for revenge among a group of violence-prone coal miners. The rest of the fatal story of this organization is picked up on April 14, 1874.

April 23, 1869—A convention was held in Worcester, Massachusetts, to formally create the Knights of St. Crispin, initially a secret organization of shoemakers that started to form "lodges" in Milwaukee in March of 1867. It was an organization doomed from the start because its main purpose was to keep skilled shoe craftsmen from being replaced by unskilled workers using a new machine. The machine (the McKay stitcher) had been developed in response to the increased need by the government for sewed shoes to supply the troops during the Civil War (one of the first times volumes of shoes were made separately for the left and right feet). The Crispins took on the aspects of a secret society in the belief it would help them succeed in trying to prevent the teaching of new employees to use the new machinery. As has happened to all organizations formed to prevent the spread of new technology, the "Crispins" collapsed after being unable to support the strikes needed to prevent the use of the new technology in non-union operations in the industry. The Crispins almost disappeared in the early 1870s before the organization turned to a new policy of cooperation. But it was still unable to halt the flow of unskilled workers into its industry, and it finally just became another footnote in the history of the organization of labor in the United States.

December 28, 1869—Once again the idea of a labor organization starting out as a secret society occurred to a developing labor organization called the Knights of Labor. They were started at the end of 1869 in Philadelphia by a group from a collapsing garment cutters' benefit society. The driving force for the Knights of Labor was Uriah Stevens, a mason who had been originally trained in the ministry. He was able to provide much of the ritual for the new secret society, designating local unions as "local assemblies," five of which could become a "district assembly." Eventually, a "general assembly" evolved, and it would have elected officers (some of whom were only socialist or ritualistic in function), and this assembly would have a key executive to guide the national union the Knights were trying to form. His title was the "Master Workman." This was the post to which Stevens was elected.

The Knights of Labor grew gradually, and by 1873 it had 80 local assemblies, all in different local trades. As a severe depression began to spread in the 1870s, members from other ex-unions began to join because the secret nature of the society allowed them to avoid the union "label," which many employers wanted nothing to do with now that jobs were tight and union-bashing came easy in such times. In a quiet way the Knights of Labor established assemblies in Illinois, Indiana, Ohio, and West Virginia as well as in its "home" state of Pennsylvania. Uriah Stevens was still the "senior" District

Master Workman in District Assembly Number One in Pennsylvania, but as rival districts were chartered in other states that were just as large as Number One, it was clear there was a need for another level of general authority.

Accordingly, a general convention was held in 1878, and Stephens was elevated to "Grand Master Workman" with a secretary-treasurer and a general executive board with five members beneath him. Perhaps more importantly, among other innovations, a per capita tax was imposed on all members to be paid to the general executive. This was a certain sign that the new organization had to be taken seriously. It would have money to actually carry out its plans. But one further change was needed. For several reasons the secret nature of the society was now becoming a handicap rather than an advantage. One of those reasons was the fact that the general public began to associate secret societies with criminal activity. We'll pick up the story of the end of the Molly Maguires next, and then come back to the ongoing progress of the Knights of Labor.

April 14, 1874—An employee of the Pinkerton Detective Agency named James McParlan was initiated into the Ancient Order of Hibernians at the home of Michael Lawer in Port Carbon, Pennsylvania. Of course no one there knew McParlan was a "Pinkerton," or he would have been killed on the spot. The Molly Maguires were all members of the Hibernians, an Irish benevolent society, but there was supposedly no real connection between the leaders of the two groups. The Mollies made decisions locally and carried out their crimes with local (or imported) killers. In a way the Mollies were a small-scale Irish version of the Mafia, which would become notorious in the United States in the next century. The Mollies were not in any way a union organization, but sometimes a particularly vicious supervisor would be targeted for "action" by some angry Mollie.

Franklin Gowen, President of the Philadelphia and Reading Railway, who had been very active in negotiations with the now-defunct Workingmens Benefit Association, took the lead in stopping the reign of terror by the Mollies. In October 1873 he met with Alan Pinkerton, head of the best-known Private Detective Agency in the United States at that time, and they agreed that McParlan, himself an Irish immigrant, was the right man to infiltrate the Mollies and gather the needed information to prosecute them.

Late in 1875, John P. Jones, a local mine foreman, was killed by two gunmen, Edward Kelley and Michael Doyle, who were directed by James Kerrigan, who was in hiding. These three men were later arrested, and Kerrigan confessed and agreed to turn state's evidence. Doyle was brought to trail in Mauch Chunk, Pennsylvania, on January 18, 1876, and found guilty on February 1, 1876. Seven more persons were arrested soon after for other murders, and even though it became generally known that Kerrigan was providing evidence, and, although McParlan himself came under suspicion, McParlan was able to keep gathering information.

At the trial of the second gunman, Edward Kelley, Kerrigan's confession finished off Kelley, and Kerrigan went on to claim that these murders and other acts of violence were done at the direction of the Ancient Order of Hibernians, at least as reflected through the Molly Maguires. The Mauch Chunk trials were creating a sensation in the newspapers, and when the scene shifted to Pottsville, Pennsylvania, the courthouse was jammed. On May 4, 1876, at Pottsville, five more men were convicted. McParlan revealed his double role, and he also claimed that the Ancient Order of Hibernians were the true source of evil in the anthracite coal region. Alex Campbell, a local leader of the Hibernians as well as a saloonkeeper, was convicted of taking part in two other murders with his friend, Thomas Munley.

In the end, nineteen Mollies were hanged after their appeals were exhausted. Ten alone were hanged on June 21, 1877, six in Pottsville and another four in Mauch Chunk. The last of the 19 men were hanged by January 16, 1879. Others were jailed for perjury and for being accessories before the fact. In some places the Mollies became legends of labor. But the hard facts are that they were a secret group of killers and that many of their crimes reflected simple ethnic hatreds (not to mention that they often killed each other). Their only connection with labor was that they sometimes killed supervisory personnel who worked in the mines. In the long run they did no good at all, but they unfortunately helped usher in a period of violence in the history of the labor movement in the United States.

July 6, 1877—A strike broke out on the Baltimore and Ohio railroad in Baltimore when the freight division refused to accept a pay cut. This was a strike that ignited a series of railroad strikes throughout nearly the entire northeastern section of the nation. The whole series of strikes generally became known simply as "The Strikes of 1877." Generally, the unions ultimately lost the strikes, but the public became greatly concerned about the frequency (and occasional violence) associated with strikes on such a fundamental national resource as the railroads.

As the strike wound its way along the Baltimore and Ohio lines, Governors called out their militias and President Rutherford Hayes was convinced to send in the troops to keep the trains moving. What could best be described as a comic opera followed, except that dozens of people were being killed. Local militias and National Guardsmen tended to side with the strikers rather than crack down on them, and some federal commanders arrived drunk and unable to function as the strikes spread throughout Pennsylvania. Then New York trainmen joined in, and clashes between strikers, their sympathizers, and strikebreakers and soldiers were taking place everywhere in a very chaotic manner.

All of this was happening mostly during the month of July. In Ohio some steel makers joined the railroad workers on strike, and the same kind of thing happened in Indiana. When the strikes rolled into Chicago, the crossroads of the nation, officials became more intense in calling for both local and federal troops. By July 27, trains were beginning to roll again. When problems started in St. Louis on July 22, troops appeared in force and the problems ended by July 28.

The results of this month of essential anarchy were that the people were disturbed to find that the same problems could happen in the States that had been happening in Europe. It was the first time that Federal Troops had been called in to intercede in problems of this type, and this was a precedent the unions would have cause to regret. It certainly suggested some effort was needed to be sure fair negotiations were held between capital and labor, but the net result was that the general public now felt a sense of unease about the growing number of unions in the United States.

January 1, 1878—This was the date of the 1878 convention of the Knights of Labor that closed the entry for December 28, 1869. The issue of secrecy became a contentious one, with Catholics being put into an especially difficult position because the Catholic Church disapproved of secret societies in general and specifically of certain quasi-religious elements in the rituals of the Knights of Labor. Uriah Stevens, still the number one man in the Knights, and a Protestant, did not want to make concessions on the question of secrecy. Further, Stevens had temporarily retired from his post as Grand Master Workman in 1878 to run for Congress on the ticket of the Greenback Labor Party (which managed to win over a million votes total in 1878), then came back to the Knights in 1879 and was elected to his former post. However, he soon resigned permanently in 1881 over the secrecy issue, and was replaced by Terence V. Powderley, a Catholic born of immigrant Irish parents.

Powderley's greatest contribution in office may have been securing Vatican approval of the organization in 1888, and opening membership to members of all and any trades and industries, as well as welcoming minorities and women, at least in its pronouncements. Powderley believed in the concept of cooperation and questioned the use of the strike as an economic weapon. He much preferred the use of the boycott. The Knights grew rapidly after they abandoned the secrecy requirement, growing from about 19,000 members in 1881 to 110,000 in 1885. It appeared they might become the first truly national federation of unions. But Powderley was basically a weak leader, and although he remained Grand Master Workman until 1893, it seemed he was often willing to make compromises rather than taking the strong stands needed to keep the Knights a viable organization. As a result new contenders for national labor leadership quickly appeared. Many union activists felt that a strong national representation was needed to enable unions to achieve their goals.

August 2, 1881—A convention was held in Terre Haute, Indiana, to consider the establishment of a new national labor federation. The officers of the International Typographical Union had persisted over the last several years to bring such an event about, and they were a guiding force behind the conference. The Amalgamated Labor Union of Terre Haute also played a key role as it was one of many labor unions at the time looking for a national organization (the depression of the 1870s had given way to better times and it was a good time for unions). The International Typographical Union was considered a "pure" union, i.e., they did not pursue national social goals or the formation of political groups (but they were willing to work for legislation that would be favorable to their agenda). They primarily concentrated on obtaining benefits for their members in the areas of better wages and working conditions. The initial attendance at the August meeting was discouraging, and the prime result was a call for a second meeting to be held in Pittsburgh on November 15, 1881. This next meeting would turn out to be a turning point in labor organization.

Samuel Gompers, who had been active in forming and leading a union of cigar makers in New York, came to the Pittsburgh conference. He was one of many union leaders who felt the Knights of Labor were not suitable to lead a national effort, even though they approved of some of the policies of the Knights. Terence Powderley, the leader of the Knights, was very suspicious of the intents of the new group, and he tried to pack the meeting with delegates favorable to him. But John Jarrett, head of the Amalgamated Association of Iron and Steel Workers, was named Presiding officer, and Gompers quashed rumors that he was there to "steal" the conference for the Socialists by withdrawing as a candidate for permanent chairman when Jarrett was nominated for the post from the floor. Gompers then worked carefully behind the scenes as chairman of organization, and "The Federation of Organized Trades and Labor Unions" was born. It grew very slowly, but by 1883 Gompers was chosen to preside over its convention. He was moving up as he bided his time.

May 1, 1886—Originally proposed in 1884 by the new Federation under Gompers, this was the date selected as the day of the inauguration of the eight-hour days for all trades. Even though a series of successful strikes had driven the membership of the Knights from 110,000 in 1885 to over 700,000 a year later (it would grow to over a million shortly after), Powderley was characteristically cautious as the day neared, and he sent out a secret circular saying he was not ready to support the strike. The unions struck anyway, and it appeared initially that they were successful. But as has happened so often in union history, the unions decided to take a mile instead of an inch, and disaster was the result. The employees of the stockyards struck first, and after the eight-hour day appeared to be attained, they made another demand relative to working conditions, and it was refused and a pay cut was made in response. When this was refused in turn, the employers decided to reinstall the 10-hour day by October 11. Strikes broke out accordingly. T. B. Barry, an executive of the Knights, was sent out by Powderley with instructions not to involve the Knights in the controversy.

It so happened that another strike was taking place in Chicago at the same time. A long strike against International Harvester had recently been broken by the hiring of replacement workers who were being protected by the Chicago Police and Pinkerton Detectives. Gompers made a speech to union members at Union Square, but events were about to overtake him. On May 3 a group of strikers attacked the replacement workers, and the police responded with gunfire that killed or wounded six strikers. On the evening of May 4, a mass meeting was held in Haymarket Square to protest the shootings. The speeches went on without incident, but as rain began to fall the police began "helping" the attendees break up the meeting and go home. Arguments broke out, and someone threw a bomb into a mass of policemen. One was killed instantly and six others died later. Many were injured. The police fired into the crowd and some fired back, and a total of ten people finally were killed and scores were injured.

What became known as the "Haymarket Riot" ended a decade of violence that had existed between labor and law enforcement in the years between the Molly Maguires of 1875 and the summer of strikes in 1877 and the present. The conclusion of the American people, rightly or wrongly, was that there lurked in labor organizations a criminal element capable of anything. In the minds of most, the results of the Haymarket Riot bore this out. In a month indictments were returned against 10 anarchists, one that was arrested and released and never seen again (later he was identified as the bomb-thrower by some witnesses). By August one anarchist had turned state's evidence, and the remaining eight were found guilty, with seven sentenced to hang. After appeals were refused, pardons were requested. Ultimately four were executed in November of 1887, one committed suicide before hanging, and two were pardoned.

"May Day" is a celebrated holiday in many countries around the world. No such event is held in the United States. No one in the States wanted to "celebrate" the incident in May by designating it a holiday. Essentially, what would be May Day in the States is Labor Day, which had first been started locally in New York in 1882, and then elevated to a National Holiday by President Grover Cleveland in 1894 to wipe out the remembrance of the Haymarket Massacre of 1886. Gompers tried the May 1 approach for an eight-hour day again in 1890, but it failed again after an initial success. The May 1, 1886, day is considered the proper day by most.

May 13, 1886—Samuel Gompers was quick to see that the Haymarket affair could be an important turning point for labor. On this date a special meeting was called by the Federation of Trades to resolve a long festering battle between specific trade unions and the Knights (many held memberships in both organizations, and the issue of "dual unionism" was a hot topic in all unions). The Knights held meetings on May 25, 1886, and October 4, 1886, to consider what was essentially a list of demands from the trade unions (that would essentially put the Knights out of business). It took the Knights some time to find members willing to form a committee to deal with the explosive issue, and Powderley finally had to appoint the general executive board of the Knights to do so. The Knights in October finally decided the only solution was for the Knights to disassociate themselves from the Cigarmakers Union, which was leading the other side (although the cigarmakers were also battling internally between the "socialists" and the issue of "dual unionism" on one side and the group controlled by Gompers on the other side).

December 8, 1886—Gompers, as seems to be true for all men who turned out to be leaders in the first 175 years of the United States, sensed that now was the moment for dramatic action. In a meeting called in November to respond to the edict of the Knights in October, it was decided that the existing Federation of Organized Trades and Labor Unions needed to be leaner and meaner to deal with the crisis. Accordingly, the old Federation was dissolved, and a new federation called the American Federation of Labor (AFL) was created to succeed it, with Gompers as President. Except for a loss of the Presidency in a battle with the Socialists in 1894, Gompers was President of the AFL every year of its existence from 1886 to 1895, and from 1896 until his death in 1924. In one stroke, Gompers had left only the Knights of Labor to be tarred with the brush of the Haymarket incident, and this black mark was one of the reasons the Knights began their drift downward to oblivion. The AFL would rule the world of organized labor until the CIO was torn from its ranks in 1938.

January 1, 1887—Gompers began his first full year as president of the AFL (in his twenties he constantly said he would one day form the leading national labor organization and he would be its president) in the "central office" of the AFL. It was one small room, provided rent-free by his local cigarmaker's union. It was furnished with a box for a chair. The full staff consisted of Gompers and his son Henry, who was hired as office boy at three dollars a week (Gompers had 10-12 children—he claimed never to be sure of the number because only four lived to be as old as forty). Gompers' official salary of $1,000 a year (a good wage then) did not officially begin until March, but Gompers was anxious to begin his new job on any terms, because he felt it was his life's calling.

Gompers had a priceless store of ideas and the conviction that he had been preparing for this job all of his life (he was 37 years old, and still had 37 years to live). While he was involved in leadership positions with his local union, he watched carefully what made some unions fail and some succeed, and he had very definite ideas about what a union should do and should not do. He was truly the right man at the right time for the job. There is no way to soften the fact that he was in many ways a bigot, and he made his share of mistakes of the "often wrong but never in doubt" type, but Samuel Gompers, and his hand-picked successor, William Green, held the labor movement together until the Roosevelt Administration rode to the rescue in the 1930s.

In short, Gompers believed that unions should avoid getting entangled in social movements (specifically like the Socialists); they should build themselves "horizontally" on the basis of skilled craft organizations; they should avoid being used to further the political ambitions of any person or party; and they never undertake to delay the introduction of new technology to protect jobs—they should rather cooperate in the introduction of new technology in a way that would help union members share in the benefits generated by the gains produced by the technology. The new technology would win no matter what and the smart play was to be on the side of the gains it would bring. What he wanted to give the unions was better wages and working conditions, period. Gompers was often quoted as saying what unions want "is more and more, here and now." That was what he was going to give his members, and he was going to avoid the other paths of "pie in the sky" that had undermined so many other unions. Gompers was short on furnishings in his new central office, but he was not short on brains, and he had an iron will.

The constitution of the AFL gave him little real power, and it was up to him to get things done by sheer force of persuasion. But he believed that each individual union in the Federation had to feel it was autonomous in terms of its own self-government. Then it would feel free to join the Federation to gain those advances only a united front could produce. This way the AFL would avoid "the fatal rock on which on all other previous attempts at ... unity have split" because the affected organizations did not feel completely in control of their own affairs. Gompers was an accomplished writer and speaker, and he was sure he could do the job, even if he had only an empty box and his son to begin with.

December 5, 1888—While Gompers was nearly single handedly enlarging the AFL membership by writing thousands of letters telling unions how to organize, and exhorting the advantages of affiliating with the AFL (Gompers started by traveling about 25,000 miles in a year, riding immigrant trains and cabooses, spreading his ideas both on the trains and in the literally dozens of cities where they stopped). A very important union was coming to fruition in very difficult conditions.

As noted in the entry for January 28, 1961, a coal miners' union was a very desirable goal among coal miners. A major difficulty was that the United States was rich with coal, and there were coal-mining regions spread throughout the nation. Further, (hard) anthracite coal is nearly pure carbon and is more desirable for domestic heating. It was mined mainly along the Appalachian Mountain chain from Northern Pennsylvania into Alabama, which is why Pennsylvania quickly became one of the top coal producing states. Bituminous coal is softer and burns with less efficiency, and thus is most often used for fuel in industries because of its lower price. A further complication is that certain states, like West Virginia, have coal that is relatively easier to access and that tends to grow in thicker seams, giving the state an inherent competitive advantage.

As if all these variations were not enough, the enormous railroad boom in the later 1800s meant that each mine was actually competing with mines all over the states because their coal could be relatively easily brought to any market once it was loaded on a railroad car. Good times in the nation meant a huge demand for coal. Once the United Miners Union was founded on this date, it grew to the largest single union in the states by 1897, and it held that position for almost the next three decades. It is easy to understand how John L. Lewis wielded immense power once he became President of the union in 1920.

Many references show 1890 as the year the United Miners Union was formed. But on this date, December 5, 1888, a united union called The National Progressive Union of Miners and Mine Laborers was formed out of several unions that had been calling for unity for a long time. Its only opposition was District Assembly No 135, one of the still-surviving parts of the Knights of Labor. At the convention of the National Progressive Union in the 1890, the President of the Progressive Union took the lead in calling for a final unification, and he graciously agreed for the key positions of president and the secretary treasurer of the new union, now called the United

Mine Workers of America, to come from the unions in the convention that were affiliated with the Knights. What's more, the leaders of the Knights, including our old friend President Terence V. Powderley, opposed the merger, and continued to fight against it for a few more years. This is why December 5, 1888, is shown as the true birthday of the United Mine Workers. They changed their name in 1890, but the men who created the union in 1888 were the true leaders and founders. The Mine Workers were an Industrial ("Vertical") union, but still they affiliated with Samuel Gompers' rapidly growing AFL. These two organizations, with many struggles along the way, would keep organized labor alive until the 1930s.

July 2, 1890—On this day Congress passed the Sherman Anti-Trust Act (named after Senator John Sherman). It was intended to attack trusts such as those assembled by Rockefeller, but Sam Gompers cautioned against the early celebrations held by many of his friends. He read the Act as applying to any organization that could be defined as acting in restraint of trade, and he forecast it would one day be applied to unions. He was right.

July 6, 1892—At early dawn a force of some 300 Pinkerton detectives were loaded on two barges and towed up the Monongahela River by a steamer named "Little Bill" to their destination at the Homestead Steel works near Pittsburgh. Striking union members were tipped off about its arrival, and a gunfight ensued between the Pinkertons on the barges and the union members on the shore. Initially two Pinkertons and two union members were killed (some reports finally claimed a dozen deaths on each side, and others claimed 7 Pinkertons and 11 union members and onlookers, and another source claimed 3 Pinkertons and 9 workers). After a few hours, a new landing was attempted. The Pinkertons were hopelessly exposed, and when the Little Bill tried to retrieve the barges, it was driven off and oil spread on the river by the strikers in hopes they could set the barges afire. They also threw dynamite at the barges but missed. The Pinkertons raised a white flag which was ignored for some time, and when they were finally promised safe passage they had to run through a gauntlet of strikers on the shore.

The strike was supposedly about, among other things, the company's insistence on changing the renewal date of the contract to January 1, when it was hard for the union to consider striking, from its present July 30 date, when strikes were easier to consider. The strike was really mostly about the union's hatred for H.C. Frick the prior owner of a coke factory who had sold his business to the Andrew Carnegie Corporation and had become one of Carnegie's trusted supervisors. It was no secret Frick was out to break the union. The Sons of Vulcan had called 87 strikes between 1867 and 1875, while the Amalgamated Steel Workers had succeeded them with 93 strikes between 1876 and 1885. This was part of the reason company owners across the nation were out to take a hard line in the 1890s.

After the governor sent 7,000 troops to Homestead, the strikers were forced off the premises. The troops remained until October 13, 1892. In the meantime a young anarchist, named Alexander Berkman made his way from New York to Pittsburgh, got into Frick's office, and shot and stabbed him twice. Frick held him off until help arrived. One of the men in the troops cried out for three cheers for the man who shot Frick. After refusing to apologize following a day spent hanging by his thumbs, the soldier was courtmartialed and drummed out of the Corps. This was a serious mistake because public sympathy was against the soldiers. The anarchist was given 25 years for attempted murder (he served 14 years).

In this emotional atmosphere, 167 strikers were indicted under one law that carried a $2,000 fine and 12 years imprisonment and under other laws, and three were charged with murder. Among others, Samuel Gompers spoke in their defense. Except for two men, all on both sides were found not guilty or had their indictments dismissed. Two men were convicted of assault and battery because, in their role as cooks, they had tried to poison the nonunion men in the mills.

But the real aftermath of the Homestead strike was that hundreds of union men were locked out of their jobs, and the Homestead Plant did not operate under any union agreement for the next 45 years. A union was kept for the convenience of the plant owners, but the steelmakers had served notice they were to be masters of their plants. Many AFL members felt Gompers should have done more, but another instance of employers taking a hard line against unions was not long in coming.

June 30, 1893—On this date the American Railway Union was formed with Eugene V. Debs as President. Debs had been a leader of the Brotherhood of Railroad Firemen, but he decided an industrial (vertical) union was needed to serve all railroad union workers rather than the craft (horizontal) union he had been leading. Debs would become a committed Socialist, and he eventually ran for President of the United States in 1908, 1912, and 1920 on the Socialist Party ticket. Although in jail in 1920 for his efforts against World War I, he still managed to pull nearly one million votes.

Debs won a short strike against the Great Northern Railroad the following April, and, brimming with confidence with a membership greater than the four operating unions combined, his union called their first convention for June 1894 in Chicago. But it became involved in the infamous Pullman Strike just before the start of its convention, and the ultimate result was the first step towards extinction of the union, not to mention a six-month jail term for Debs.

May 10, 1894—Following a meeting on May 7 with 43 representatives of all shops of the Pullman Company, and two of its Vice-Presidents, Wickes and Howard, another meeting was held on the 10th by the union employees and Howard to review the status of their ongoing dispute with the company. Howard and the union's chief officers thought that, when the meeting was over, they had convinced the men not to walk out. But the sentiment for a walkout was widespread and that's just what the unions did. This set off what would become a significant defeat for the union movement.

The Pullman Company was owned by George M. Pullman who, in 1859, developed the idea of converting railroad coaches to facilitate long distance travel. Five years later he came up with the sleeping car and it was an immediate success, bringing him great wealth. In 1880 he built the town of Pullman, near Chicago, for both his company and its workers. At one point the company declared its paternalistic town was producing a superior type of workman. No one had to live there to work at the Pullman Company, but workers easily noticed that those who did seemed to be assured steadier employment. The problem that was coming to a head in 1894 was that wages were being cut, but rents were not being reduced. The members living in Pullman soon "owed their soul to the company store," and new hires not choosing to live there were getting more than their share of shorter hours.

Debs, the new hero of the unions, was called upon to help, but the company refused to negotiate with him because his union represented members who no longer were working for the Pullman Company (having been fired and replaced). The union threatened a boycott, and got the same answer. The American Railway Union under Debs was persona non grata at Pullman. In addition, the General Managers Association, a voluntary group drawn from the 24 railroads that served Chicago, which oversaw such services as switching cars, loading and unloading them, and setting rates for services, was opposed to any boycotts.

But the union went ahead with the boycott. On June 26 a switchman refused to couple a Pullman to a train, was fired, and all other switchmen subsequently quit. By July 1 the trains were paralyzed. The General Managers Association took the lead getting deputies appointed to guard the trains as well as recruiting replacements for the strikers. As the trains began moving again, violence broke out. When some mail trains were delayed, the end came quickly into view. The U.S. Postal Service contacted the Department of Justice, and before long the Sherman Anti-Trust Law was being used as the justification for sending federal troops to Chicago (Gompers was being proved absolutely right in his prediction that the law would ultimately be used against the unions). The troops arrived on July 4. The riots spread on July 5, and several persons were killed in clashes between rioters and marshals. President Cleveland sent more troops on July 8 and issued a proclamation for the rioting to cease. The troops left after 15 days when relative calm was restored.

On July 8 a conference of unions was held in Chicago, and Sam Gompers was requested to help find some basis for settlement. The unions called for a general strike by July 10 if the issue was not resolved. The strike was called, met with little response, and, among others, Debs was arrested and placed under bond for ignoring the injunctions that were part of the court actions calling for Federal Troops and invoking the Sherman Anti-Trust Act. That ended the abortive general strike. Gompers and Debs met on July 12 and Debs requested that Gompers tell the General Managers Association that his union would call off the original strike if they all were taken back to work. Debs was asked to go along to answer any questions and confirm his willingness to end the strike on such terms (which would be an admission the union had lost the strike). Debs declined to do so. The strike went until August 2, with the railroads attaching mail cars to trains as a device to use the force of the federal injunctions to avoid interference with operations. The unions called off the strike and Pullman resumed full operations shortly thereafter.

The strike was a devastating loss to the unions, especially the ARU that Debs founded. The union lasted only a few more years. The Supreme Court upheld the local courts in every step of the process, and the companies had a new tool to use against strikers. The AFL was criticized because Gompers did not agree to carry Debs' petition to the General Managers Association, but it is hard to see what good Gompers could have done on his own when Debs refused to go along to the meeting (Debs claimed he feared a hostile reception by the members of the Association.)

Both men suffered personal defeats. Debs went to jail in Illinois to serve his six month sentence on January 8, 1895. Gompers failed to win re-election as President of the AFL when the Socialists and industrialists gathered forces to elect John McBride, President of the United Mine Workers (one of the few industrial unions affiliated with the AFL), as the new President of the AFL at the 1894 convention. McBride immediately moved the headquarters of the AFL to Indianapolis. It was the only time in his lifetime that Gompers lost. But in his "sabbatical year," Gompers visited trade unions in England and Western Europe, worked as an organizer for the United Garment Workers, gave his unending string of lectures, and lobbied everywhere for re-election. He won in the closest vote in AFL history (1,041 to 1,023) at the Denver Convention in 1895, and he never lost again.

July 4, 1897—The early part of the 1890s were a difficult time for the nation generally and unions in particular due to an ongoing depression. And although business conditions improved in the late 1890s, organizations such as the National Association of Manufactures (NAM) were formed specifically to oppose unions. Speaking for similar organizations, the NAM (formed in 1895) stated that "organized labor does not place its reliance upon reason and justice, but on strikes, boycotts, and coercion. It is, in all essential features, a mob knowing no master except its own will. Its history is stained with blood and ruin.... It denies to those outside its ranks the individual right to dispose of their labor as they see fit—a right that is one of the most sacred and fundamental of American liberty."

It was against this kind of developing opposition to unions that the United Mine Workers (UMW) made some gains near the end of the decade that propelled them to one of the most influential unions in the nation (and still the biggest single union affiliated with the AFL). Membership in the UMW had fallen from 17,000 in 1894 to under 10,000 in 1897, and even then many of the newcomers were Slavic and Italian immigrants. With the demand for coal finally growing in 1897 as the depression eased, the union decided to try to increase wage rates which had fallen by nearly half between 1893 and 1897, depending on the size of the coal vein being worked. Coal operators responded by offering more reductions.

A walkout began on this date, July 4, 1897, in the northern bituminous fields (the entry for December 5, 1888, describes the different kinds of coal mined in the United States and their most common locations), and all bituminous miners were invited to join whether or not they were members of the union. Over 100,000 miners joined the walkout, once again to the surprise of nearly everyone, and the northern fields were paralyzed. West Virginia, with its much easier accessibility to the coal seams, especially the more desirable thick ones, responded much less favorably.

Gompers called a meeting of nationally known labor leaders in Pittsburgh and personally led an effort to create public sympathy for the strikers and to raise money for their cause. Eugene Debs and what was left of the Knights of Labor tried to help in West Virginia, and the result was a blizzard of injunctions against the strikers, with union organizers being run out of many communities. This was a pattern that would continue for decades in that state. West Virginia wanted to develop bigger markets for its inherently cheaper coal, and wanted no part of strikes of any kind, whatever their alleged merit.

Negotiations for a settlement were begun in August. The final result was barely approved by the miners who were negotiating, but in January, 1898, a final agreement called The Central Competitive Field Agreement was put into effect. Not holding out for every issue originally demanded (except union recognition if that was at issue) became a characteristic of the miners and Gompers. This enabled them to get settlements where none appeared possible and to keep their memberships growing.

Parts of Illinois refused to accept the agreement, and several large operators erected blockades against black strikebreakers imported from the south. Battles with guns broke out in several places, notably Pana and Virden, Illinois. Following the deaths of seven miners and five guards, with about eight wounded on each side, the governor intervened. Finally, the strike at Virden was settled in November, 1898, and the strike at Pana settled almost a year later in October, 1899. No further effort was made in Illinois to operate with nonunion labor until what became known as the Herrin Massacre in 1922.

Overall, the strike was a great success for the United Mine Workers (and Gompers). The fact that Gompers and Union President John Mitchell were able to work so well together so soon after Mitchell had handed Gompers his only defeat as President of the AFL in 1894, and Gompers had taken the job back in 1895, was a very good sign. The strike brought thousands of new members into the UMW (and the AFL), assuring that both would remain prominent in their areas for the next three decades. The only sour note was their inability to get West Virginia, and its unique cheap coal position, to be receptive to the union. But the results of the strike in the bituminous fields gave the union the standing it needed to address a massacre in the anthracite fields.

September 10, 1897—This was the day of the so-called Lattimer, Pennsylvania, Massacre. Not many people remember it today, but more people were killed in this incident than in any of the famous battles that later took place in the west, including that of Ludlow, Colorado. The anthracite district in Pennsylvania was where the Molly Maguires had operated in the 1870s, when the mines employed over 100,000 mostly English-speaking people from the United States, Canada, the British Isles, and Germany. By the end of the century Slavic speaking people had increased from about 2,000 to almost 90,000. The coal operators had taken advantage of this to stop union organization, pay cheaper wages to the Slavs, and to organize paternalistic institutions like (high priced) company stores and company doctors.

A group of miners, marching from Hazelton to Lattimer to aid a strike specifically against a wage cut and the paternalistic practices, were shot at point-blank range by the local sheriff and his deputies. They killed 19 people and wounded 39. A jury voted 10–2 that the killings were wanton and that the marchers were unarmed and marching peacefully, but because the jury was not unanimous, the sheriff and his deputies were set free. Massive funeral demonstrations were held after the Massacre to keep emotions alive, and the UMW (and the AFL) started planning an organization drive in the year of 1900, but they knew they would have to do a lot of preparation to keep public sentiment on their side.

September 17, 1900—On this date, the miners walked out in the anthracite area. Their leaders had started the process at their convention on August 13 by drawing up a list of 12 issues to be resolved, and they even proposed to accept the results of arbitration. The response to the strike by the non-represented miners was once again pleasing to the union leaders, and for such a strike violence was minimal with only one spectator being killed and one special guard being wounded badly enough to later die.

In the meantime, Gompers got help from the fact that 1900 was an election year. Mark Hanna, dubbed the Republican Kingmaker, had been a prime mover in creating in 1900 an organization called the National Civic Foundation (NCF). It was composed of union leaders (like Gompers, who was vice president), businessmen (like Hanna), clergymen, judges, and Wall Street figures (like August Belmont, and, on call, the original great J.P. Morgan). The NCF was essentially a vehicle for conciliation, following Belmont's edict that it was generally much cheaper to settle strikes quickly than be drawn into an all-out war. Even Andrew Carnegie's position before the Homestead affair was to accept unions and deal with them (which is exactly what he did after the disgruntled owners, tired of dealing with worker issues, sold Homestead cheap and then watched Carnegie make peace and make profits). Many big businesses agreed. The most profitable way of operating those gigantic factories was to keep them churning out product full time.

The NFC thought the Homestead mess cost the Republicans the presidency in 1892, and they wanted no repeat performance in 1900. An agreement was reached that brought the union a wage increase of 10 cents per hour, but no union recognition. The miners wanted to stay out, but Mitchell and Gompers continued their "half-a-loaf" policy that had been successful so far. When they got the operators to agree to extend the increase through April 1, 1901, and to end the sliding scales in the Schuylkill and Lehigh regions, the workers went back to work on October 29, 1900. It was a strike of just over two months, and one with no violence on the part of the strikers, who, at that time, were the biggest group ever to take part in a strike in the United States. It was a solid victory for the strikers, assuming they consolidated it with recognition. The union tried to get their consolidation in March and April of 1901, but even with the help of the National Civic Federation and a special input from J.P. Morgan, the best the unions could do was to extend the agreement until April 1, 1902, and get an agreement that the operators would agree to discuss employee's grievances with their committees.

The workers were beginning to lose patience as 1902 brought more of the same. The operators refused to meet on March 12, 1902. The union upped the ante with a request for an eight-hour day with no loss of pay. A 30-day "cooling off" period was held, and then successive postponements were made. By a narrow vote the miners agreed to go out even though their President Mitchell was opposed. He felt he could make more gains without risking everything on a "make-or-break" strike. Mitchell pleaded that peaceful methods be followed. He recognized the need for the public's support.

The workers went out in May, and little violence took place in the first month. Pressure was brought on Mitchell to shut down the bituminous mines as well. Mitchell had to call a convention to discuss the issue per the constitution of the union, but on July 17, 1902, he called for strong financial support for the anthracite strikers rather than breaking the contracts of the bituminous workers and going on strike. The strikers fell on hard times as the strike continued, but Mitchell was able to point out that his union kept to its contracts and the public responded favorably. Violence began to appear as the strikers ran short of supplies, and by the middle of September, 14 people had been killed. President Roosevelt declined to get involved even though people were beginning to worry about the thought of winter without coal for heat. Roosevelt realized his most likely intervention would be on the side of the operators to protect the mines, and he wanted to avoid that.

But by October 3, 1902, Roosevelt felt he had to act. A typical government council with a cast of thousands was assembled, and John Mitchell immediately agreed to binding arbitration by a tribunal to be assigned by President Roosevelt, but the operators refused. The next step was to call out the National Guard, but not surprisingly, this failed to increase coal production. The union was seen by the public as taking a much more reasonable and flexible stance than the operators, and public sentiment swung more strongly to the side of the union. Finally J.P. Morgan appeared behind the scenes again and a commission of seven was appointed to arbitrate differences while the union returned to work. The operators almost scuttled the agreement by imposing unacceptable terms, but Mitchell kept the plan on track, and by October 21, 1902, Mitchell told the union to return to the mines.

The commission walked a narrow path in giving something to each side. The breaking point was the recognition of the union, which the operators would have nothing to do with. But Mitchell accepted a statement in the settlement which read "that a plan, under which all questions of differences between the employer and his employees, shall first be considered in conference between the operator or his official representative, and a committee chosen by his employees from their own ranks, is most likely to produce satisfactory results and harmonious relations, and at such conference the employees would have the right to call to their assistance such representatives or agents as they may choose, and to have them recognized as such." It's not clear what the operators thought this would lead to, but to Mitchell it was as clear a grievance procedure as one could wish for, as well as a statement that the union was recognized as the ultimate arbitrator for the miners. It was spelled "victory" if it was desired to state it in a different way.

This victory in the anthracite fields was a "tall pole" in the history of organized labor. By their willingness to (apparently) accept less than their total demands, the union gained an impregnable place in an industry that was determined to keep them out. The union had gotten its nose under the tent and they would not easily be removed without wrecking the tent. Membership in the union grew from about 11,000 in January 1898 to approaching 250,000 in July 1901. The United Mine Workers were not only an important source of new recruits for organized labor (the AFL), but for the next 20 years they propped up the entire labor movement. As long as Coal was King, they were King.

December 31, 1902—When the final numbers were in from 1900, it was clear that coal was indeed king in terms of providing energy for the booming growth of the nation, now the world's biggest and richest as measured by industrial output. As immigration continued, the United States had 76 million people by 1900. Coal production grew from 43 million tons of bituminous coal to 212 million in 1900, and for anthracite coal the corresponding numbers were 30 million tons to 57 million tons. Mitchell had timed his coal strikes just right. The demand for coal was rising to new highs.

Pig iron output rose in the same period from less than 4 million to over 10 million tons. Steel production jumped by a factor of 8, from 1.25 million to over 10 million tons. The railroads were so busy that employment for just the decade starting in 1890 rose from 750,000 to over a million as the new century began. The nation was indeed booming.

Sam Gompers kept the AFL booming as well. Craft union or not, he worked out ways for the Mine Workers and Brewery Workers, both Industrial Unions, to become affiliated with the AFL, and these two unions were among the top six in the AFL in terms of members. In spite of the financial panic of 1893, which led to a depression in the following four years, the AFL fought off all challengers. In fact, these tough conditions may have helped the AFL in the sense that it was a bad time for a new union organization to get established. Even the new Sherman Anti-Trust Act (aimed at monopolistic corporations when it was enacted in 1890) was used in the 1894 Pullman Railroad Strike to essentially kill a new union started by Eugene Debs (see entry for May 10, 1894) and put Debs in jail for six months. Gompers had predicted this, but it wouldn't be until the turn of the century that he would find it used with devastating effect against the AFL.

With the United Mine Workers reaching a membership of over 100,000 in 1900 and then growing past 200,000 in 1901, the AFL was nearing a total of one million in 1901, nearly three times as large as it had been as recently as 1898. Its main competitor, the Knights of Labor, were not more than 200,000, and they were on they way to expiring after hooking their star to the Populist Party, and the Populists evaporated after doing badly in the 1892 and 1896 elections (one researcher said the Knights made the fatal mistake of strapping themselves to a cadaver). Another confirmation of a Gompers edict to avoid outright ties to a political entity.

So life looked good for the AFL as the new century started. The percentage of the work force that was unionized was estimated to be seven percent, a new high. The AFL had grown from 264,000 in 1897 to 548,000 in 1900, and then past one million in 1901, and on to 1.7 million in 1904. But the AFL was still mostly composed of craft unions, and their failure to organize more industrial unions would hurt them in the years immediately ahead. They would stall at the 1.7 million number until after World War I, and storm clouds in the form of the Industrial Workers of the World (the IWW) and others were gathering.

January 2, 1905—This was a date that led directly to a change in the labor movement, a change that put the movement into a state of flux for the next 15 years. On this date a secret conference was held in Chicago to call for yet another conference, one that, with the aid of the Western Federation of Miners, would call a convention to help create a new federation based on what was known as "dual unionism," an approach to a labor federation that was anathema to the AFL and its followers. The new federation was expected to replace the AFL, and any other pretender for that matter.

The Western Federation of Miners was organized on May 15, 1893. It arose out of several groups that were initially associated with the Knights of Labor. It primary included Metalliferous Miners (those who mined ores containing gold, silver, copper, etc.) rather than coal miners. These miners wanted industrial (vertical) organizations rather than the craft (horizontal) organizations like the AFL, with whom the Western Conference of Miners associated in 1896. Many miners carried membership cards in two unions, one of each type, hence the name "dual unionism." Samuel Gompers claimed this was nothing more than an attempt to defeat the power of labor by the ancient method of "divide and conquer," but the proponents of dual unionism, many of whom leaned heavily towards the Socialists, said it was the only way to address their special needs. One of the dual union leaders, Eugene Debs (see entry for June 30, 1893), was a powerful leader at this time, and brought much credibility to the Federation's desire for a dual union. He ran for president of the United States in 1900 on the Social Democratic Ticket and drew nearly 100,000 votes. After a merger, the official name of the party was changed to the Socialist Party in 1901, and Debs would run as the Presidential Nominee of the Socialist Party in 1904, 1908, 1912, and 1920 (in 1920 he was in jail, and he still drew about a million votes).

As usual in the west, differences between the unions and operators almost always led to violence. Names like Leadville, Colorado; Coeur d' Alene, Idaho (twice); and Cripple Creek, Colorado (twice); became infamous in the later 1890s and early 1900s for attacks by unions on non-union strikers brought in to break a strike, and the following escalation of violence when troops were brought in to stop the violence. The few persons actually brought to trial were usually found not guilty by sympathetic juries, even when the former Governor of Idaho, Frank Steunberg, was assassinated by a bomb planted at his home on December 30, 1905. In this case the Western Federation of Miners had a member who confessed to being the "chief terrorist" of the Federation. He said he was hired as an arsonist, dynamiter, and terrorist by the "inner circle" of the Federation. He even confessed to murdering 26 men in dynamiting a mine and a rail station. As the trials plodded along, the Governor of Colorado authorized the kidnapping of the top executives of the Federation, William D. "Big Bill" Haywood and Charles H. Moyer, from Denver to stand trial in Idaho. Such was justice in the west in those days. Labor was enraged by the incident, and even Samuel Gompers, no friend of either Socialists or dual unionism, came to their defense. As usual, all defendants were eventually acquitted of everything.

It was against this background that the Western Federation, at a conference on May 10, 1898, helped organize the Western Labor Union as an organization to eventually serve in place of the AFL. The Western Labor Union moved its headquarters from Denver to Chicago in 1902, renamed itself the American Labor Union, and set out to beat up on the AFL. It accomplished nothing. The next step was the January 2, 1905, secret conference held in Chicago primarily among Socialists who wanted to take over from the AFL. They wanted "one great industrial union" to take the lead. They planned a convention from a selected list to discuss their agenda in Chicago on June 27, 1905. This convention turned out to have momentous results.

June 27, 1905—The most important delegates at this conference were those from the Western Federation of Miners. Also, a number of known Socialist and radical leaders were invited to represent themselves as were some smaller Socialist organizations. The leaders at the conference were William "Big Bill" Haywood from the Western Miners Federation, Daniel de Leon, a key Socialist Party leader, Eugene Debs, and Father Thomas J. Haggerty, editor of the official organ of the American Labor Union. After 11 days the conference gave birth to a new labor organization called The Industrial Workers of the World (IWW). C. O. Sherman was named President, and W. E. Trautman Secretary-Treasurer. Both were from the Western Federation of Miners, as was Charles Moyer, a member of the executive board of the new organization. He had been President of the Federation.

June 27, 1905

This date is known as the birth date of a new labor organization, the IWW, but it could just as well be described as the birthday of a new Political Party dedicated to the overthrow of the U.S. Government and anything else having to do with things as the were in the States. Big Bill Haywood began proceedings by proclaiming that the delegates were at the birth of a second American Revolution, and told his "fellow workers" that "this is the Continental Congress of the working class." Haywood was consumed by the idea of class warfare, and a decade later he would almost surely doom the IWW, which wanted no part of World War I, by saying that "that it is better to be a traitor to your country than a traitor to your class." It is no accident that the first line of the preamble to the constitution of the IWW states that the "the working class and the employing class have nothing in common." The concept of the IWW was that everyone would join "one big union," and at the proper time a general strike would be called that would bring the country to its knees. The IWW leaders would then take over all governmental agencies, and union workers would take over all business enterprises. The means of production would then be run by the IWW to satisfy social needs rather than private profits.

The day-to-day plans of the IWW were just as fanciful. They wanted low dues and fees, and no check-off systems by employers to collect what dues there were because this insulated the workers from the union leaders. No deductions for health and welfare were planned because the coming social revolution would solve these problems, including special collections for emergencies. There would be no written contracts with time boundaries so employers could not take advantage of them. Unions would simply strike whenever they felt the need for "more," and union solidarity would be sure to make all strikes winners. The IWW also mumbled loudly when asked if they approved of violence, but they did favor "sabotage," and they needed no mumbling to agree they favored massive civil disobedience to any law they found to be, in their opinion, unjust.

Despite such impractical planning, the IWW did have one unquestioned success in a textile strike in 1912. However, their methods of operation converted even that quickly to a non-event when no IWW representatives stayed around to follow-up (no written contracts). They assumed once fixed, always fixed. But the IWW spent most of the time between their founding in 1905 and the 1912 strike arguing about their real aims and who should run what based on who was "purer" than who. There is not much more to describe between 1905 and 1912. The biggest losses of the IWW were Eugene Debs, who left the organization in 1906 (he decided it was basically an anarchist organization), and the loss of the Western Federation of Miners, once the biggest supporter of the IWW, who also left in 1906 due to the disputes over organization, goals, and leaders. In 1912 the IWW saw more changes.

March 18, 1908—A "Protest Conference" was held on this date and attended by many unions. The conference was called by the AFL to protest a decision by the Supreme Court in a case called the "Danbury Hatter's Case." The case began in 1902, when the Hatter's Union struck Loewe and Company, a maker of hats. They also had a boycott, as was common then, telling people not to buy Loewe's hats. Loewe sued under the Sherman Antitrust law (as Gompers had forecast would happen some day when the law was passed in 1890. The law had also been used in the Pullman Strike in 1894, but few seemed to notice that the Supreme Court upheld its use then). In 1908, the Supreme Court affirmed that the union had lost the case based on the Sherman Act following a series of appeals. The protest conference led to new trials in October 1909, where the unions argued for an amendment from Congress to protect them from the Sherman Act on the basis they were not engaged in trade or commerce. In August 1912 the amount of the award given to Loewe and Company was settled by a unanimous Supreme Court. Another issue was that the union members themselves were found liable, not just the overall union. Finally, in 1916 the AFL raised enough money to pay the fine for the individual members. The total bill for whole case cost the labor movement $421,477, an enormous sum at the time. The case was another blow to the union's ability to battle with employers.

December 23, 1908—Along the same lines, but with serious personal implications for Gompers himself, another event took place while the Hatter's case was progressing through the courts. In a case involving a strike at The Buck's Range and Stove Company in St. Louis, Gompers, on the advice of his counsel, placed the company's products on a "We don't patronize..." list and ignored an injunction obtained by the company. The result was that on this date Gompers, the secretary of the AFL and John Mitchell, the second vice-president, were sentenced to one year, nine months, and six months in jail respectively for contempt.

There were the usual appeals, complicated by the fact that James Van Cleve, the head of the Buck's Range and Stove Company, died in the meantime. His death led to an amicable settlement of the strike between the unions and the company. The Supreme Court said the issues were moot with the end of the strike and sent the case back to the original judge without any ruling. When Gompers and the other defendants refused to apologize for their actions, the original judge reimposed the sentences. Another appeal went to the Supreme Court who found that the statute of limitations barred punishment and dismissed the case. The defendants were displeased because they felt the basic issues had not been ruled on. They had lost the secondary boycott issue in the Danbury case, and they now had to stop using the "We don't patronize..." list anymore based on the Range and Stove Company case.

They also realized that companies were actively developing strategies and forming groups to get rid of unions. The National Association of Manufacturers (NAM) had already appeared on the scene in 1895, and new organizations such as the Citizen's Industrial Association, the National Council of Industrial Defense, and the American Anti-Boycott Association were organized in the first decade of the 1900s. They all proclaimed the evils of unions, and created strategies and assistance for companies who wanted to be rid of them and/or their adverse (to employers) effects. The problem was about to get worse for unions.

October 1, 1910—On this date the *Los Angeles Times* building was destroyed by a bomb and 20 persons lost their lives in the resulting fire. This followed a long battle between the *Times* and several unions because the *Times* supported an open shop policy (as opposed to a closed shop policy where all workers have to belong to a union). Also involved was an organization called The Erectors Association which was an anti-union group working in the building and construction field, and the Iron Workers Union, which was involved in bitter disputes with The Erectors Association and the American Bridge Company.

The Iron Workers Union immediately came under suspicion because since 1905 there had been 95 instances of dynamiting or attempted dynamiting on non-union projects of the American Bridge Company. At the time of the explosion, there was an escalation in the battle between union and non-union shops, with the *Times* recognized as the beacon for non-union shops throughout California. The California State Federation of Labor did a quick investigation blaming the *Times* for its anti-union behavior and claimed the *Times* was trying to create another "Haymarket" case. No one not in a union believed anything the Labor Board claimed, and the city and several manufacturers' associations began their own investigation.

Finally, John J. McNamara, secretary-treasurer of the Iron Makers union, and a man named Ortie McManigal, were arrested on suspicion of the crime. Governor Hiram Johnson of California secretly signed extradition papers to get McNamara from union headquarters in Indiana to California. This happened on April 22, 1911, and with assistance of a local court that did not necessarily have the authority to act on the case, McNamara was taken away to California. In the meantime, Walter Drew of the National Erectors Association, who was invited to go on the trip to Indiana, spent a great deal of time examining the files of McNamara because an executive meeting was going on when the group from California burst into union headquarters to serve their papers. The attendees were held temporarily as prisoners and another executive council member was also taken to California.

Unions everywhere protested the proceedings, and the AFL took over the defense. The infamous Clarence Darrow was asked to take the case and handed $200,000 from the funds many unions had raised for a "fair trail" of McNamara, who was painted as a gentlemen and a scholar by everyone with a union card. Jury selection began on October 11, 1911, and slowly proceeded until the real "bomb" in the case was dropped on November 28, 1911. An investigator for the defense was arrested for trying to bribe a juror, and three days later McNamara and his brother, John, the other man taken from the council meeting in Indiana, pleaded guilty. James, the original suspect, pleaded guilty to murder, and his brother, John J. to conspiracy in the dynamiting of another facility. The inner members of the defense agreed Darrow had suggested pleading guilty because he felt the evidence was strong enough that both men might otherwise end up on the gallows.

Their pleas of guilty resulted in a term of life imprisonment for James McNamara and 15 years for John McNamara. A Federal jury indicted 51 more men, 47 of them members of the Iron Workers Union, for conspiracy to transport dynamite and nitroglycerine. All of these were tried in Indiana, and Ortie McManginal, who confessed to 22 dynamite jobs under the direction of John McNamara, was the chief witness. Of those put on trial, all were found guilty. Five received suspended sentences; seven got a year and day; and the rest got seven years in Federal prison.

Perhaps the saddest case was that of Clarence Darrow that wrapped up the California part of the trials. He was accused of trying to bribe two jurors (and suspected of diverting some defense funds for his own use). He was acquitted in one trial, had a hung jury in the second, and returned to Chicago with his reputation in tatters. But his most famous trials (and successes for him) were still to come.

January 11, 1912—General strikes broke out at the textile mills in Lawrence, Massachusetts, under the direction of the IWW. This action is probably the most favorable impression the IWW made on the general public in its roughly 15 years of useful existence. The basic issue was how a reduction in schedule from 56 to 54 hours for women and minor children, who made up most of the work force at the plants, would affect wages. A big division existed in the work force between the skilled members of the United Textile Workers and the IWW, which claimed to represent essentially everyone else. By January 14 the mostly unskilled polyglot workers who spoke at least six languages, elected Joe Ettor, an organizer for the IWW, as chairman of the strike committee. The strike demands escalated to a 15 percent increase in wages, double pay for overtime, elimination of the bonus system, and no discrimination against strikers. The battle was on.

Troops arrived on January 15, 1912, and much was made of the discovery of dynamite in a tenement until it was found to have been planted by

John Breena, a local businessman, to discredit the strikers. Big Bill Haywood showed up to support his IWW, and on January 29 Anna Lo Pezzi was killed by shots from a revolver in a battle between strikers and police. Joe Ettor, the strike leader, and Arturo Giovanitti, an Italian Socialist who had been active in the strike, were arrested and charged with first-degree murder. The strike committee started having children sent to other cities to persons sympathetic with their plight, and the city fathers of Lawrence made several attempts to stop what they saw as a slur on their city. After 30 people were arrested in a riot on February 24, 1912, in another attempt to move children out of Lawrence, the city fathers of Lawrence realized they were doing more harm than good to their city, and made no more attempts to stop the children. But it was too late.

A storm of indignation had arisen to the extent that resolutions were being introduced in Washington to investigate the strike in Lawrence. John Golden, head of the United Textile Workers was so unnerved by the possibility of the IWW overriding his union that he made a statement saying he found it just fine for the police to be interfering with the IWW. This brought Gompers into the act, because the Textile Workers were affiliated with the AFL. Gompers said in essence that Golden must be suffering from temporary insanity brought on by stress, and he, Gompers, was sorry the AFL was affiliated with the Textile Union. He said the strikers had a right to do whatever they saw necessary to do to carry on the strike, and that certainly included moving their children to safe havens.

On March 19, 1912, the American Woolen Company made an offer with definite wages for definite jobs. The strike committee recommended acceptance, and the workers were back in the mills almost exactly two months after they walked out. During those two months 296 persons had been arrested, some with more than one charge. That left 355 cases to try. A total of 220 were fined, with the fines ranging from $1.00 to $100.00 (only 40 were fined more than $10.00). More seriously, 54 were sentenced to prison, with 27 receiving one year, and the maximum time for anyone sentenced was two years. Ettor and Giovanitti were acquitted of their murder charges in November 1912. For a struggle involving thousands of workers that were mostly foreign, and one that attracted nationwide attention and a generous settlement, it had to be rated a smashing success by anyone in the organized labor business.

But there was one major defect. Most IWW leaders looked on strikes as propaganda devices to have new members sign up across the nation for "their one big union." No functional IWW union organization was left in the wake of the IWW blitz. Now that the workers had been shown how, they were expected to carry on the hard organizational detail by themselves. This happened time after time with the IWW, even after they shifted their focus to the west, with its mines, and harvests, and seaports. They made lots of noise with their "free speech" marathons and their famous songs, and they probably had more romantic nonsense written about them than any labor organization ever to arise in the United States. But they dared the government to do anything about what IWW leaders said and did relative to World War I, and when the government took the dare the IWW was destroyed. We will pick up this part of the IWW story after World War I.

October 15, 1914—President Wilson signed the Clayton Act on this day. It was the result of a long effort by Gompers, turning away from his self-imposed edict to avoid political entanglements after he lost his boycott cases, and lobbying individual Congressmen as well as the President with an ardent, full-press style. Gompers went to press (prematurely as it turned out), praising the Clayton Act as labor's Magna Carta, because the act seemed to exempt labor from the parts of the Sherman Anti-Trust Act that had been burying unions in injunctions and greatly hampering the actions of labor. However, starting as early as 1917, courts began declaring the Clayton Act unconstitutional, voiding the protections the unions saw there, not to mention other items impacting child labor laws. A separate Child Labor Law enacted in 1916 was also thrown out in the same year as unconstitutional. As discussed in the introduction, no law is final until the Supreme Court decides on its validity, and the Clayton Act was essentially destroyed by the Supreme Court (as were other acts in the early 1930s) that promised labor some relief.

April 6, 1917—The United States formally declared its entry into World War I on this date, partly ending the honeymoon Washington and Gompers had been having since the Clayton Act came to fruition. Gompers had become the key spokesman for labor in Washington, and, with the passionate support of the AFL in 1916 to reelect Wilson, Congress and President Wilson were passing laws favorably addressing most of the famous "Labor's Bill of Grievances" Gompers had submitted to Congress (and President Theodore Roosevelt) in 1906. The AFL had vanquished all of its rivals by 1914 (except perhaps the IWW), and it was a good time for both Gompers and the AFL, which grew to 2.4 million members by 1917. The increased demand caused by World War I for munitions by other countries and then for the United States itself, while immigration was cut off by the war, made more jobs available, which always helps the outlook for organized labor and most other workers. As part of the advisory council on the National Council of Defense, as appointed by Wilson, Gompers became an active supporter of the War effort, a role labor usually had eschewed in the past. He also continued to be a hard and astute bargainer for his unions, and with money pouring into the war effort, the AFL grew from its 1917 peak of 2.4 million to a membership of 3.3 million in 1919. Life was good for the AFL.

September 17, 1917—It was around this time the IWW reached its peak, and was about to tumble into the abyss. Estimates of the peak membership in the IWW range from over 100,000 in 1918 to as much as 250,000 after the war ended. But this higher number was a government estimate and also surely too high because the government wanted to scare citizens about the potential of the "Wobblies," as they were popularly called, to damage to the country. At best, the IWW claimed a peak membership of less than three percent of the AFL.

It has never been fully explained how the name "Wobblies" came into existence. One story says it was due to the odd tilt given to the "WW" in their hand-written signs. Another oft-told story says it was due to a Chinese immigrant on the west coast, who rushed into a gathering preparing for an expected march by the IWW, shouting in the best English he could manage, that "the Wobblies" were about to arrive. The name stuck because the IWW itself felt it softened its image.

It was an image that could use some softening. With Big Bill Haywood as their leader since 1914, the IWW started to raise money by focusing on the migratory workers who moved from harvest to harvest, living in hobo "jungles" and the like. At first the money was raised by request, but then the Wobblies turned to pure extortion. As most migratory workers moved long distances by illegally "riding the rails" of freight and other long distance trains, the Wobblies forced such workers to "line up" to join the IWW and pay for the famous red cards symbolizing IWW membership. Otherwise they were dumped from the trains. Similarly, those railroad employees who were told to enforce the law by their employers and eject the illegal riders were pointed out to the Wobblies, and when enough Wobblies could be assembled to easily overpower the one employee trying to enforce the law, he would be severely beaten. Many Wobblies themselves objected to such strong-arm tactics, but the IWW had stumbled upon a sure-fire fundraising tactic, and they didn't want to give it up. The IWW now focused on migratory workers in several areas like those in the agricultural and lumbering fields, and the IWW made more of an impact in 1915 and 1916 after they had acquired some money. None of these activities found their way into the rallying songs the Wobblies were famous for.

Joe Hill (or Hillstrom) was a well-known writer of these songs, but became more famous for songs written about him. Hill was convicted of the murder of a storekeeper and his son on January 9, 1914, during a robbery outside Salt Lake City. It was naturally claimed that he was railroaded because of his radical ideas. At the time of his arrest, Hill carried a bullet wound, which he attributed to a fight over a woman. After Hill was sentenced to die on July 6, 1915, Gompers and the AFL joined a campaign to get President Wilson to commute the sentence. Finally, the Governor of Idaho and its pardon board promised a reprieve if Hill would tell two of its members where he was the night of the shooting, which had been an issue in the trial. Hill refused and was finally executed. He instantly became a martyr for the cause, and folk singers still sing sad songs about him today. But there was good evidence of his crime.

The IWW was active in several strikes during the war in spite of labor's general agreement to refrain from strikes that would hurt the war effort. The IWW had made it known that it felt no obligation to support the war because they saw it as a capitalistic issue no worker should support. Big Bill Haywood's statement that "it is better to be a traitor to one's country than to one's class" came back to haunt him and the IWW. On September 17, 1917, IWW halls were raided by government officials, and a number of IWW leaders were indicted for conspiracy to resist the war effort. Federal statutes enacted on February 3, 1917, and October 16, 1918, made aliens deportable if they were anarchists or believed to be in the overthrow of the government by force and violence (as the original IWW constitution could easily be read to encourage). Eventually a number of organizations came into being after the war to punish those who harmed the war effort, and the IWW was targeted by many of them. The IWW then made a fatal error in strategy.

Haywood urged the members to meet the attacks head on by turning themselves in and agree to the government's plan for a mass trial in Chicago. He believed that most of the charges were fabricated and that even President Wilson was opposed to the trial. George Vanderveer, counsel for the IWW, predicted a slam-dunk win in an "all or nothing" fashion that would have immense propaganda value. Elizabeth Gurley Flynn, a nationally known speaker and organizer for the IWW, opposed this approach. She proposed making the government prove its case against every single defendant. The longer the case took, the more it would fester in the divided camps in Washington, and the further the war hysteria would fade into the background. It could take years to serve warrants and win extradition against those who fought it. Her ideas were right but, because she was a woman, were not seriously considered. Women were gladly welcomed into the IWW, but not in decision making positions.

The two persons in addition to Flynn who followed her course eventually had the charges against them dropped. The rest who went for "all or nothing" in 1918 got nothing (except for the 46 who got temporary freedom on bail). Some were sentenced to up to 20 years and their fines up to $20,000. When all appeals were exhausted by April of 1921, Big Bill Haywood showed his leadership qualities by jumping bail (along with eight others). Haywood fled to the sanctuary of the new Soviet Union, where he ultimately died and was buried in the Kremlin Wall along with other Soviet "heroes." Before he died Haywood offered to return to the United States if those who had forfeited his posted bond money were reimbursed. But the government and he could not come to terms.

Even as the IWW was in its death spiral, quarrels broke out as to whether some jailed Wobblies should accept pardons. The "pure" approach (held mostly by those who were out of jail) was that accepting a pardon was an admission of guilt, and a good Wobbly, as a "class war prisoner" should accept a release that resulted only from the direct action of his fellow (free) Wobblies. When some Wobblies did accept clemency of some type to get out of jail, other "pure" Wobblies (who never went to jail) ostracized them as class traitors. It is sometimes hard to decide if the IWW was a functioning labor union organization or a philosophical debating society. When Haywood visited national headquarters while he was out on bail and saw the depth of the discord going on, he was reportedly heartbroken and dazed at what had happened to the organization he had put his adult life into. Perhaps that is why he was willing to take his chances with the legendary intrigue in Moscow compared to the nonsense going on within his once beloved IWW. The convention of 1924 is usually taken as the official end of the IWW, with the group splitting in half and one side suing the other regarding the rights to the remaining property.

The remnants of the IWW became ever more anarchistic, and even as late as World War II they remained on the "subversive" list. They were romanticized beyond belief by radicals in the 1960s, but by the early 1980s, the IWW newspaper had a monthly circulation of about 3,000, with due paying members in the hundreds.

April 1, 1922—This date marked the beginning of what became known as the Herrin, Illinois' Massacre. The cycle had become all too familiar by now. Non-union workers were brought in by an operator, William J. Lester, to ship coal during a strike. Private guards were brought in to protect them, but after a series of small clashes, the union miners attacked the mine. The guards and strikebreakers surrendered, but emotions were now so high that the men who had surrendered were beaten and shot. Eighteen were killed. And this time, public opinion appeared to be on the side of the strikebreakers since most were killed after surrendering. Forty-four miners were charged with murder, 58 for conspiracy, 58 for rioting, and 54 for assault with intent to murder. In addition, the company operator and the sheriff were indicted for their actions in permitting things to get out of hand. Of these 214 indictments, only nine men actually ended up standing trial, and all were acquitted.

This was essentially the initiation of John L. Lewis as head of the United Coal Miners Union, although there were other strikes on his watch before Herrin, as unions generally came under attack after the end of World War I and through the 1920s. Lewis had worked in these mines as a teenager (as did his father). He worked his way up the ranks of the union, becoming president of his local at age 29 in 1909, then an AFL organizer (with which the coal miners were affiliated). When the president of the Miners Union moved on to another job in the Federal Government in 1917, the resultant shifting of places left Lewis as acting Vice-President to new President Frank Hayes. When Hayes resigned in the fall of 1919, Lewis became acting president and simply slid into the president's spot when no opposition to Lewis developed. Lewis was 39, and spent the next 40 years in the job. By 1933 the United Mine Workers were the most powerful bloc in the AFL, and Lewis later became the head of the CIO (the Committee of Industrial Organization), which became the Congress for Industrial Organization when he took it out of the AFL in 1938.

Lewis was no shrinking violet from the beginning, challenging Samuel Gompers for the Presidency of the AFL in 1921 on the basis that Gompers was no longer up to the job at age 71. Lewis was actually correct (Gompers died three years later), but the AFL was not ready for a whirlwind like Lewis, especially as Lewis was pushing industrial organization as opposed to the traditional craft organization of the AFL. Lewis claimed the coming growth industries of automobiles, oil and refining, steel, chemicals and so forth would be best organized as industrial organizations like his own miners' union. He was absolutely right, but it would take another decade for him to prevail. If Gompers was the leading labor figure at the start of the labor movement, Lewis would become the leading labor figure in the middle, irritating friend and foe alike until he ended his run friendless and irrelevant in the 1950s, dying in near obscurity when he was 89 years old in 1969. But if there had been no Lewis, there would have been no CIO.

December 13, 1924—Samuel Gompers died in Laredo, Texas, during a trip made to Mexico City to support labor relations between Mexico and the United States. He was 74 years old and had been increasingly fragile and in poor health in the preceding years. He was replaced by William Green, secretary-treasurer of the United Mine Workers, keeping a key union in the AFL well represented in its leadership. Green was a good friend of John L. Lewis, but a firm disciple of Gompers. Green was the son of a miner and started in the mines himself at the age of 16, the same story Lewis could tell. Green also worked he way up to president of his local miners' district in 1906 at the age of 33. But Green then moved into political office, serving in the Ohio Senate from 1911 to 1913, where his major accomplishment was improving the Workmens Compensation law. The Miners Union then called him back and he served there until moving up to the top of the AFL in 1924, when Gompers died at 74 while Green was 51.

The AFL was struggling somewhat when Green took over, partly because Gompers had lost his fire due to the infirmities of old age, and partly because unions were under attack throughout the 1920s. The four million members at which the AFL had peaked in 1920 were down to under three million in 1925. They would be near the same at the end of the decade even as employment boomed well into 1929. Green was a faithful leader, but not one in the dynamic mode of John L. Lewis, or even Gompers for that matter. But Green would guide the AFL through the fateful 1930s and the schisms of the breakaway CIO. The AFL would be a thundering success when Green died in 1952, as compared to its somewhat precarious position when he took over in 1924. Green deserves his position as one of the top labor leaders of the century.

March 23, 1932—President Hoover signed what became known as the Norris-La Guardia Act after Senator George W. Norris of Nebraska and Representative Fiorello H. La Guardia of New York (later to become mayor of New York and to become famous for, among many other things, reading the funnies to children, and probably many adults, during a newspaper strike so that everyone could follow the exploits of their favorite cartoon heroes). This was the first of many pro-union bills to pour out of Washington in the years ahead. The fact that both of the act's sponsors were Republicans and that it was passed by overwhelming margins were signs that the Republicans knew what was coming in the November elections, and many were anxious to distance themselves from "Dead Man Walking" Herbert Hoover.

The Act, which is still in force today, limits the power of the government to issue those hated injunctions against unions (in fact, it is also sometimes called the Anti-Injunction Bill). It had a defect in that it only applied to federal courts, but in years to come many states would pass "little Norris-La Guardia acts." The executive council announced that the act "really represents the outstanding legal accomplishment of the AFL." Chalk one up for new AFL President William Green. The AFL had been trying to push the act through Congress for a little more than five years. It would turn out to be a small umbrella against the unemployment deluge to come, but it was a step in the right direction. And the AFL was the first labor organization to get a bill favorable to unions passed while Hoover still ruled.

March 4, 1933—The next major event in the labor movement, and perhaps its most seminal event ever, was the inauguration of President Franklin Roosevelt almost exactly one year after the Norris-LaGuardia Act was passed. Roosevelt began the first few of his famous "First Hundred Days" with a focus on saving the collapsing banking system, delivered his "first fireside chat" on March 12, and then turned to the crisis in unemployment. By the end of 1932, unemployment was estimated to be between 12 and 13 million, some 25% of the work force. The driving force for the pragmatic Roosevelt was that whatever the system was it was clearly broken, and it was time to try something else—fast.

There is no doubt that the Roosevelt Administration brought great changes to the manner in which organized labor and management dealt with each other, and the changes primarily favored the unions. The unions finished the war in 1945 in their most powerful and prosperous condition ever. But before we deal with how these changes came about, and who were the prime movers on both sides in accomplishing them, it has to be said that perhaps some of the most important players in the game between 1933 and 1945 were not in Washington, or even in the United States. They were in Berlin, in the person of the mad wallpaper hanger named Adolf Hitler, and in Tokyo, in the persons of the militarists who pretended to permit the emperor to rule while they called the shots. Even with the all the changes in the manner in which the unions and companies would deal with each other, the favorable results of these changes would have been far less dramatic for the unions if World War II had not followed quickly upon the "labor law" changes.

The wartime needs for munitions and other products for both the allies and the Unites States, plus the need for men and women in the United States military, increased total manpower needs in the country by 10 million between 1940 and 1944. The gap was made up by essentially reducing unemployment to as close to zero as possible, while increasing the total number of women in the workforce from 11 to 17 million, an increase of over 50 percent (6 million). After Pearl Harbor the United States was in a condition of "overfull employment" for the duration of the war. With plenty of money available for overtime, the unions were in a good state with jobs available everywhere and new rules acting in their favor. Union membership grew from a record 8.7 million in 1940 to 14.3 million in 1945, representing 35.5 percent of the workforce in 1945. This compared to 3.4 million union members in 1930 representing only 11.6 percent of the workforce. It was World War II that pulled the United States out of its long depression, and that gave the unions a condition of unparalleled prosperity. The unions didn't know it then, of course, but the year following the end of World War II in August 1945 to the Congressional elections in November 1946 marked their peak for the century.

May 17, 1933—President Roosevelt sent a message to Congress proposing a plan for national recovery. The plan was called The National Industrial Recovery Act (NIRA). The plan was to permit companies in an industry to establish "codes" of "fair practice" against which workers and the company could bargain collectively without running afoul of anti-trust laws. The first so-called "code" (in the Cotton Textile industry) was approved July 9,

1933. There was much more in the NIRA, and William Green and John L. Lewis had testified extensively for the AFL in the hearings held on the NIRA since it was proposed by President Roosevelt. Section 7 (a), which addressed the rights of unions to collectively bargain as the representative for employees who voted to have a union, was especially dear to the hearts of all union organizers. The key concept of the government expressed in the act was that it had accepted that workers would be better off with unions to bargain with management for them, and it had established detailed procedures for employees to create (or not create if they so wished) unions to bargain on their behalf. Unions reported great increases in organized members, with the AFL gaining 800,000 members by October 1933, just since the act went into effect after June 1933. But friction between the unions and management was building as everyone was trying to learn how it would work, especially with respect to Section 7 (a) which covered union elections for representation.

August 5, 1933—President Roosevelt set up a National Labor Board under the chairmanship of Senator Robert Wagner of New York to deal with the problems that were arising from implementation of the NIRA. Because the Board's recommendations were often ignored, a National Labor Relations Board was established by President Roosevelt on June 29, 1934. Problems continued, but at least each side was learning what the pluses and minuses were, and how to work the system in their favor. Even Roosevelt seemed to be even-handed when criticizing first the unions and then management as cases continued to arise.

May 27, 1935—All of the arguments about the NIRA seemed to become moot when the Supreme Court struck it down as unconstitutional. But Senator Wagner was not about to give up so easily. He introduced a bill called the National Labor Relations Act on February 21, 1935, to address what he saw as the defects in the NIRA, and debated drones in Congress even as the NIRA expired in the Supreme Court. Unfair Labor Practices were carefully defined, and the experience gained from trying to make the NIRA work was factored into the new bill. The House and Senate Bills finally passed were different, and they had to go to conference to get a bill sent to the President.

July 27, 1935—Just two months after the NIRA was killed by the Supreme Court, a new bill covering similar ground was signed into law, The National Labor Relations Act (now often simply known as the Wagner Act). Most eminent counsel at the time said the bill would never get past the Supreme Court. Even 25 years later, the first chairman of the National Labor Relations Board (which was reborn in the Wagner Act), Judge J. Warren Madden, said that he knew that most members of the board would privately advise that a client, if asked for their advice, should ignore the bill because it had no chance of being upheld.

But in its first test case in April 1937, The Supreme Court upheld the Act by a vote of 5-4. The unions had won, and they could now enjoy the fruits of victory. However, the unions had some internal problems of their own to digest first. It is amazing in retrospect how many basic issues came to the fore for unions in the year 1935.

November 9, 1935—The AFL Convention, which was held on October 7, 1935, in Atlantic City, was primarily occupied with the ancient issue of craft (horizontal) versus industrial (vertical) unions (the organization of millions of new workers was at hand thanks to the Wagner Act). Just a little over a month later, on the date that heads this entry, John L. Lewis convened a meeting under his direction in Washington with eight unions in attendance to form a committee for industrial organization (CIO) within the existing AFL framework. This in spite of the fact that a vote on forming such a committee at the convention had been in the negative.

November 23, 1935—AFL President William Green said in a letter that he was very "apprehensive" about the formation of such a committee, even if it still was supposedly within the AFL, to try to organize new workers along industrial lines. Lewis resigned his position of AFL vice-president when the letter came out. So this date could be taken as the day the AFL and CIO split for all intents and purposes, even though more than a year of debate would continue on the subject. Lewis was then at the peak of his powers, having brought the United Miners Union through an almost disastrous decade in the 1920s. This meant he was President of the most powerful single union in the AFL, an industrial union, even though the miners had had been affiliated with the AFL for almost half a century. There was a further exchange of letters between Green and several of the heads of the other unions on the committee, and then Green wrote a new letter on December 12 saying that he felt the new committee would try to split the AFL and would have to cease and desist.

September 5, 1936—Charge and counter-charge followed during 1936. It was demanded at an AFL executive council meeting on July 8, 1936, that the (now 12) CIO unions be suspended. Lewis essentially told the executive council to take a hike because he claimed they did not have the legal authority to do what they proposed to do. This date, September 5, 1936, was the date by which Green gave the CIO to acquiesce to his demands. Subsequently, the AFL convention, meeting on November 6, 1936, approved the suspensions and appointed yet another committee to negotiate a possible settlement because Lewis said the suspensions would have to be lifted before he would discuss anything with anybody. Lewis was not really interested in a settlement. His CIO was signing up new union members at a prodigious rate. But even as late as during the AFL convention that began on November 16, 1936, after the convention had approved the suspensions, a new committee was appointed to "explore the basis for a settlement." It wasn't until the AFL Convention of 1937, held in October of 1937, the executive council was given full power to revoke the charters of the CIO unions. And even after that, a "peace conference" was conducted from October 27, 1937, through December 21, 1937, to see if the original CIO unions could be convinced to reaffiliate with the AFL. Lewis rejected all proposals unless the (now 32) unions in the CIO were readmitted on his terms. Then it might be possible to hold discussions. The game appeared to be over. One could select nearly any date between November 23, 1935, and the end of 1937 for the final split of the AFL and the CIO, but certainly by the end of 1937 there were now two active independent labor organizations, the AFL and the CIO, recruiting new members under the Wagner Act.

November 14, 1938—On this date the CIO formally changed its name to the Congress for Industrial Organization, keeping, conveniently, the same initials, the CIO. There were a lot of political wheels behind the split of the AFL and the CIO. President Roosevelt and John L. Lewis were good friends in the early 1930s. Roosevelt was interested in someone who could deliver votes in big blocks, and Lewis, as president of the then biggest single union in the AFL, had the potential to do so. Roosevelt saw the AFL as far too conservative, and made up of too many small craft unions as well to be a source of political power. Trying to get Lewis to take over the AFL was a long shot because he had an overbearing personality with many enemies who feared him and would not support him. So the logical step was to try to split the AFL.

Lewis was very ambitious and more than willing to support Roosevelt. Many suspected Lewis thought about a run for the presidency himself when the time was right, and the third term was still a no-no at the time. It was clear that the industrial workers had the biggest potential unions to be formed. Automobile manufacturing had become the single biggest industrial entity in the United States by 1929, and the United Auto Workers, Rubber workers, (five tires for every car), the Teamsters (as the trucking industry grew with the great increase in trucks on the road), and the Chemical Workers, etc., were just waiting to be organized. It was also clear these workers wanted to be organized by industry, not split up into multiple crafts. Lewis was pushing the right course of action, even if perhaps for the wrong reasons (the major concern for Lewis was the advancement of his own career). But Lewis always delivered for his union. His miners would follow his lead unquestionably. He got them the goods.

In early 1933 Lewis began to plan the CIO when President Green of the AFL declined to launch a massive organizing drive among industrial workers. Lewis made a big splash in the 1934 council and, in his eyes, the AFL council agreed to a big effort in 1935. When the AFL broke their promises, as Lewis saw it, at the 1935 convention, Lewis went out on his own. Lewis delivered a dramatic punch in the nose (supposedly planned by Lewis for maximum theatrical effect) to Bill Hutchenson, President of the Carpenter's Union, who went flying backwards over a table while Lewis calmly relit the cigar he had clamped in his teeth throughout the event. As Lewis planned, it was the talk of the convention. Everyone assumed that in another year, Lewis would win the battle. But he was in no mood to wait, and on November 9, 1935, he called the committee meeting that started the whole process of splitting the AFL as noted above.

Lewis included many communists in his organizing efforts because everyone agreed they were the best organizers. Where the established AFL told new additions to pay their dues and try to see where they could help the union, the CIO told new members just to sign-up, but there would be no dues until the CIO did something for them. Lewis just wanted those dues check-offs as soon as he could get them. When he was criticized for using the communists and was told they were using him, Lewis said, "Who gets the bird—the hunter or the dog?" The new CIO members tended to be easy to sign, but they were not very loyal and easy to steal away. However, it was not easy to talk to Lewis about methods of strategy. He never took advice from any subordinates, and he considered everyone on a subordinate level to him.

The AFL was pushed into an organizing frenzy once they saw what Lewis was accomplishing and greatly increased their membership, essentially replacing the members lost when Lewis created the CIO. Lewis was unquestionably insufferable at times. But he was a formidable opponent. Lewis essentially built the CIO from scratch and kept winning victory after victory. He overstepped himself when he broke with Roosevelt for the 1940 third-term election. It was the end of his meteoritic rise in the labor heavens, but he drove friend and foe crazy for still another decade (although many of his detractors, after criticizing him, went right out and copied his methods).

September 1, 1939—Adolf Hitler brought many matters to a head when he invaded Poland to start World War II on this date. The ease with which Hitler overwhelmed the valiant Poles made it clear that Germany was going to be able to back up its big words with big actions. On September 5, 1939, President Roosevelt proclaimed that the United States was neutral, but every country in the world knew which side the United States would eventually support.

From the standpoint of the unions they were ready to go to build up the "arsenal of democracy" that would be needed. It was estimated that nine million union members existed in the nation in 1938, one million who were in independent unions with four million each in the AFL and the CIO. The CIO numbers were surely inflated, as they held their data close to their chest, but the affiliated total was still close to triple the number of less than three million the AFL could claim in 1933. The AFL and CIO and their employers had more than two years of learning to operate under the Wagner Act.

The prime issues to resolve, as always, were political issues. Lewis and his Mine Workers had raised $500,000 for Roosevelt in his 1936 campaign. Lewis saw this as a down payment on his becoming the prime Labor Advisor to Roosevelt in his second term. But Roosevelt did not see it that way, and felt Lewis was much too volatile for such a role. The men quickly moved from friends to enemies, especially on Lewis' side of the fence.

This took the edge off some of the pride Lewis and the CIO could feel from their new "sit-down strike" technique (when the workers simply sat down in the plants and refused to leave) that won them many new members in late 1936 and early 1937, especially among the United Automobile Workers (UAW). This technique got more credit that it perhaps deserved, as everyone involved knew it was illegal, and the Supreme Court quickly shut it down. It also depended heavily on support from the public and local and state authorities, and after the novelty wore off, that also disappeared. On the plus side the technique quickly got union recognition (which the Wagner Act et al would have brought anyway), and it introduced a fiery new labor leader, Walter Reuther of the UAW, to the world of organized labor. But on the minus side it demonstrated a disturbing tendency for unions to break the law for any purpose they wished, even when the Wagner Act, including the new National Labor Relations Board, provided a legal route to accomplish their aims.

October 25, 1940—Just before the election of 1940, in which Roosevelt was expected to win the third-term victory that would break all prior precedent, Lewis came out with a radio speech that completed his break with Roosevelt, and that almost surely ended any future hopes of higher advancement in organized labor in the personal career of Lewis. The speech was a "take-no-prisoners" attack on Roosevelt for letting the country drift into war, and claiming Roosevelt was simply interested in personal power, the worst example of which was Roosevelt's pursuit of a third term, which Lewis said would be a "national evil of the first magnitude." Up to this point it was just another personal attack on Roosevelt, of which there had been countless examples in the political life of Roosevelt.

But Lewis took it another step, and here he made a great miscalculation of his own personal power. Lewis stated that if Roosevelt were reelected, Lewis would believe it meant that the members of the CIO had "rejected his advice and recommendations." He would take this as a vote of no confidence and he would retire from the CIO at its next convention in November. Lewis retired as promised, but in his usual non-compromising way. When complaints were raised that there was no mention of the presidential election in the CIO newspaper, Lewis said it was his decision and moved on to the next item. When there was criticism that although the AFL had passed a resolution of support for the resistance of the Allies in the Battle of Britain then raging, the CIO resolution on national defense ignored the battle going on in Britain and simply demanded improvement in wages and stricter enforcement of labor laws. Walter Reuther was one of the CIO delegates pushing the hardest for some sort of resolution at least recognizing the dangers of aggression anywhere. The communists would have nothing to do with a resolution that could have been interpreted as being critical of the Germans.

The communists in the CIO had gagged on the pact between Moscow and Berlin in 1939 just before Poland was invaded, but like good communists everywhere they were following the party line from Moscow, and that included saying only good things about the Axis powers. When Hitler later attacked Russia in 1941, there were more no more fervent workers for greater output of defense products from the States, than the communists in the CIO. Again, as all good communists everywhere, they followed the party line passionately even when it switched 180 degrees. This problem would haunt the CIO following World War II until a number of admittedly communistic-led unions were thrown out of the CIO, following the passage of the Taft-Hartley bill that required a "loyalty oath."

The final problem at the CIO convention in November of 1940 was the replacement of Lewis. Signs were everywhere telling him to repudiate his promise to resign and to stay instead, and no one wanted to take the initiative in bringing the subject up. Only Sidney Hillman, who had been selected by Roosevelt to the Nation Defense Advisory Commission (where he became a labor advisor in a way not much different than the post Lewis had coveted—"clear it with Sidney" became a watchword of the Roosevelt Administration), and who had helped Lewis build the CIO from nothing, had sufficient stature to do so. He came late to the convention after being tied up on government work. Lewis had attacked Hillman by name, but Hillman made a reasonable speech when he arrived, even defending his new position (to which he had been appointed by Roosevelt without requesting clearance from either the CIO or the AFL). Hillman dared to say, "when John L. Lewis steps down, there must be a demand for Phil Murray," although Hillman was careful to laud Lewis and regret his departure. Phil Murray was a vice present of the coal miners' union, who like Lewis and William Green, had been born the son of a miner, and had joined his father in the mines at a young age (10 years old in Murray's case). Murray worked his way up in the union, working side-by-side with Lewis for two decades. For a change, Lewis nominated Murray in a gracious and laudatory speech, and Murray was unanimously elected as President of the CIO. But trouble would still arise again before Lewis would give up his drive to be in command at as high a level as possible.

January 22, 1942—After the bombing of Pearl Harbor on December 7, 1941, a number of boards were set up to deal with the all-out production level needed to out-produce the axis (several such boards or committees were already operating from the preparations made during 1941 for the anticipated coming global war, and some were simply copied from what worked in World War I. Hence, a sometimes confusing mixture of names appeared before things settled down). On this date President Roosevelt established the Combined War Labor Board (also known as the Combined Labor War Board, the Combined Labor Victory Committee, or simply the War Labor Board).

Few people know that the impetus for this announcement was a letter written by John L. Lewis suggesting the AFL and CIO be put together again (he used the word "accouplement" rather than merger). William Green, AFL President, would retire and be replaced by an up-and-coming George Meany (now secretary-treasurer of the AFL) as the new head. Phil Murray would become secretary-treasurer of the merged operation. Lewis sent the letter without consulting any of the participants. Meany claimed he had never even met Lewis face-to-face, and that he (Meany) had no idea what Lewis had in mind. When confronted about sending his letter without consulting anyone involved, Lewis wrote an open letter saying that the last peace negotiation in 1939 between the AFL and CIO had been adjourned with representatives of the AFL awaiting a response from him. He was now answering that peace mandate from that particular convention, even if a few years tardy. Lewis even included a check for $60,000 as the fee for rejoining the AFL (Meany simply threw it in his desk drawer and returned it to Lewis some months later).

No one involved was sure what Lewis had in mind, but absolutely no one trusted him. Murray dutifully presented the letter to Roosevelt, and Roosevelt, wary of any interference with organized labor at what was now the moment of truth, simply merged two planned boards with three appointees each from the AFL and CIO. Lewis was not one of the appointees (at Murray's insistence), but Meany was. That was the reason for the word "combined" in some of the original titles of the board, but it finally generally became just the War Labor Board.

As an aside, Lewis' letter involved the top labor leaders for organized labor in mid-century. Other than Lewis and Murray from the CIO, everyone knew Walter Reuther was the next leader in line to move up in the CIO organization (in just a few years he would become President of the UAW as it became the biggest union in the free world). William Green (even though Lewis had identified him for retirement) was carrying the AFL torch handed over to him by Sam Gompers, and Lewis' letter further identified the person quietly moving into the top level of the AFL, George Meany. These were the "Big Six" of labor in the history of the United States, and when Lewis had been pushed to the sidelines in the early 1950s, and Murray and Green died within days of each other in 1952, Meany became the President of the AFL, and Reuther became President of the CIO. Lewis may have been a pain-in-the-neck in many ways, but he knew talent when he saw it. It's too bad his ego made it impossible for him to accommodate to the skills of other people to work together with them. The only way to work with Lewis was to accommodate to him.

May 25, 1942—Unable to get Murray out of his hair in the miners organization with the letter maneuver, Lewis took a more direct route. As noted, there was already an uproar among the communists in the CIO after Hitler made his sneak attack on Russia in June of 1941, and many of the communists reversed their course quickly after Moscow gave them the new party line. They began to vilify Lewis, along with others who existed in the CIO, only because Lewis had helped them with funds from the United Miners Union. Lewis decided to bring the miners once again close to his heart.

The International Policy Board of the CIO was called into session on this date to consider, among other issues, the empty seat of the President of the Miners Union, since Phil Murray was now busy being President of the CIO. Lewis convened a session of the executive board while the policy committee was in session, and the *United Mine Workers Journal* simply carried an announcement that the position was declared vacant because of Murray's other duties. Murray replied with a blistering attack that Lewis had used his position "to hamper the nation's victory effort," and Murray gave examples of instances where Lewis had asked Murray to fight against President Roosevelt's foreign policies. The other officers of the Miners Union felt there was no way to accept such charges and remain in the CIO. In October 1942 the United Coal Miners formally withdrew from the CIO. They were now an independent union and essentially could behave as they wished. Which, under the direction of Lewis, is exactly what they did. Lewis had them briefly return to the AFL after the war, but they left quickly again in 1947 in a battle over the loyalty oath required by the Taft-Hartley law. It was in this battle in 1947 that George Meany gave Lewis perhaps his first public dressing down in a personal debate.

From October 1942 onward, the contributions of Lewis to the labor movement were mostly negative. He was one of the best organizers and orators the movement ever had, and he built the CIO from scratch, not only becoming the first man to successfully organize on an industrial basis, but lighting a big fire under the somewhat moribund AFL to learn to organize again at the same time. When the unions stood at their peak after World War II, he had to be identified as certainly the single most important man in getting them there. But unfortunately, because of his ego and his insistence that only he knew best, he also has to be identified as the single individual most responsible for pulling labor off its perch in the form of the Taft-Hartley bill. The organized labor of today would benefit from a leader as charismatic as John L. Lewis.

May 1, 1943—Numerous boards were set up during the war to permit the unions to keep adding workers ("maintenance of membership"); to control prices and/or tie wage increases to cost-of-living increases (as in the "little steel formula"); and to continue to maintain the benefits of the Wagner Act. As has been the case in the past, the war period was a great time for unions, with generally increasing wages (including the availability of generous amounts of overtime) and full employment. Anyone wanting a job had no trouble finding one. Between 1940 and 1945, union membership grew from 8.7 million to 14.3 million, an increase of 56 percent. The percentage of the workforce that was unionized grew from 26.9 percent to 35.5 percent.

The one "catch" caused by the war was that unions pledged not to strike in any circumstance that would hinder the war effort. There were actually thousands of strikes during the war, although in most cases it was claimed the heads of the unions did not call the strikes, but rather the workers went out on their own. This would be an illegal ("wildcat") strike if the new Wagner Act was properly applied in such a case, which meant the striking workers lost many of the protections of the Wagner Act. Often the strike was brief enough that no one brought the law into effect. But the most consistent reason for strikes was the same as usual, the workers wanted "more."

On this date, May 1, 1943, John L. Lewis took the bituminous coal miners out on strike following two months of hearings and negotiations. Roosevelt took over the mines and put Harold Ickes in charge. On direct appeal from Roosevelt the miners went back to work on May 3 and new hearings were started. The miners did not get all they wanted and struck again on May 25. Another Presidential intervention was followed by Lewis calling the workers back on June 7. A directive was issued on June 18 essentially summarizing all the agreements to date. The miners found new things to complain about in the new directive and went out on strike again three days later on June 21. On June 23 President Roosevelt denounced the actions of the miners and their leader as "intolerable," and stated that from this day forward he would deny draft exemptions to miners on strike who were less than 45 years old, and subsequently requested the right to draft men up to 65 years old for non-military service. Lewis ordered the men back to work until October 31, even though Congress ultimately declined the last request.

In a new issue claimed by another set of miners, the whole ridiculous cycle of Ickes being put in charge of the mines again was resorted to before an agreement was reached and the mines returned to the operators on December 17, 1943. But a final issue still held up the return of the miners until June 21, 1944, a full year after the whole business started (and while the beaches were being stormed in France).

Congress had had enough. Roosevelt was seen as unwilling to crack down because he felt strongly that voluntary action was best, and he didn't want to push for new harsh laws. Back in 1943 many felt his threats about subjecting the miners to the draft were the result of a new law passed by Congress for which his veto was overridden on June 25, 1943, two days after he made his tough statement. It was obvious he wanted to prevent the override but Congress was fed up.

The new law was called the Smith-Connally bill (otherwise known as the War Labor Disputes Act). It required a number of new steps (although the threat to raise the non-combatant draft age to 65 was dropped as described above). But the most significant part of the bill was that it was the first anti-Labor bill passed in a generation, even with a democratic president and a democratic Congress. What's more, it had to override a veto to become law, which meant it required a super majority to pass. Many labor leaders felt they had done a great job producing the goods of war, and they were stunned when their reward was the notorious (in their view) Taft-Hartley bill of 1947. But the signs were there in 1943 that the nation had had enough of the strikes (especially for a period when there was a pledge to have none), and the strikes that rained down on the nation in 1946 sealed the deal.

September 17, 1945—With the peace officially signed with Japan only 15 days earlier, the first official strike of the post war period began with a walkout of 43,000 refinery workers in 20 states. The Oil Workers International Union (CIO) were the first to strike after the war. To put the strikes in perspective, in 1941, the last full year before the war began on December 7, 1941 (although the country was running nearly on an all-out war production basis); there were 4,288 strikes. Each strike cost an average of 5.36 million man-days of labor (one day worth of work). That's essentially our baseline.

From 1942 through 1944, after the "no-strike" pledges had been made, there were an average of 3,893 strikes per year, increasing by roughly 1,000 per year from a low of 3,000 in 1942. For these three years, each strike cost an average of 2.26 million man-hours lost. The fact that this is about 60 percent less than the baseline year of 1941 gives credence to the claim that these were not strikes generally called by labor leaders (except those like John L. Lewis), but rather strikes called by workers ("wildcat strikes"). This leads to the assumption that workers were acting on their own, without leadership in order to attain their wishes as they had presumably become accustomed to.

In 1945, as the war ended officially just as September began (the actual fighting ended in the middle of August after the second atomic bomb had been dropped), the number of strikes were nearly the same as in 1944, but the number of average man-hours lost per strike soared by 4.5 times to an average of 8.0 as compared to 1944. This showed that whole unions were now being called out. Since 1945 was partly a war year, the best comparison would be from August 15, 1945 to August 15, 1946. There were 4,630 strikes during that period (actually about 7 percent less than in 1944), but the average number of man hours lost per strike were nearly 25.9, almost 15 times as many as in 1944, and about 5 times as many as in our baseline year of 1941. The number of workers on strike grew steadily from September 15, 1945, onward, reaching a peak in early 1946. The number of man-days lost each month peaked at almost 23 million in February of 1946. This total, for just one month, was almost as high as the total number lost in the three years from 1942 through 1944. It seemed the whole nation was on strike for "more." As it turned out, everyone ended up getting almost an identical per hour increase, but some strikes were more infamous than others.

The Oil Workers, who began their strike on this date, went back to work for an increase of 18.5 cents per hour after President Truman seized the refineries and had the Navy operate them as of October 4, 1945. Many researchers saw this period between August 1945 and August 1946 as the most contentious period of labor disputes in the history of the country, but nearly everybody finally settled for the same eighteen cents an hour, regardless of their initial demands of the length of the strike.

The cost obviously unseen by the unions was the loss of patience by the American people with strikes and strikers. Many citizens compared the union workers on strike to the U.S. citizens fighting the war. Non-union citizens decided to use the power of voting against the unions.

November 21, 1945—After a few months of preliminary negotiations, the United Automobile Workers (UAW), the biggest union in the free world with 1.2 million members, went out on strike against General Motors, the world's biggest company. Walter Reuther was the vice-president in charge of the union in the plants, but everyone knew he was aiming for the presidency of the entire UAW, an objective he would win in 1946 by a narrow margin. The UAW selected GM, the giant among Ford, Chrysler, and the other smaller car makers in the hope that GM would not want to be out of production when the pent-up domestic demand for cars broke lose and GM would lose market share to their competitors.

The UAW asked for a 30 percent increase in wages, and also presented the novel idea that GM should promise not to increase prices because the UAW claimed GM could easily afford such a wage increase without raising prices. GM offered a ten percent increase, and rejected out of hand any question of negotiating on whether they could afford a bigger increase without raising prices, which the UAW immediately complained was an "unfair labor practice." Reuther believed the request not to raise prices would gain public support. But GM canceled the union contract on December 10, said they questioned whether they could afford maintenance of its union contracts in the future, and a long siege loomed ahead.

John L. Lewis had, as usual, something to say about the contract from his perspective when he was testifying before a Congressional committee. He claimed GM would actually make more money keeping its plants closed than open due to the tax refunds it would receive to cover its losses. He took the trouble to add that the "dishonesty of the company is equaled only by the stupidity of that labor organization." While Lewis had run the CIO, he and Reuther had not seemed to get along.

Truman created a board to study the issue, and said it seemed appropriate to him to look at the company's books in confidentiality since the ability to pay was always an issue, but GM said since it had not requested price relief, no one outside the company had the right to look at its books. The board reviewed the issue without GM's participation, and recommended an increase of 19.5 cents an hour. The strike dragged on, but in January of 1946 the UAW settled with Ford at 18 cents per hour and with Chrysler at 18.5 cents per hour, the increases representing only 15.1 percent at Ford and 16.7 percent at Chrysler, far under the 30 percent they had asked for from GM.

In addition, while the strike was on, a number of companies in other industries were settling at 18.5 cents per hour. The UAW finally did the same on March 13, 1946, after 113 days on strike. It was not lost on the UAW workers that they essentially got nothing out of their extra days on strike compared to companies that struck for much shorter periods of time. The issue of holding the line on prices was long since forgotten. But Reuther had more new ideas in mind for future strikes, and he would eventually devise the model for other companies to copy on non-wage issues.

May 17, 1946—President Truman took the railroads over on this date following the failure of negotiations that had been ongoing since July 1945.

After long investigations government boards came up with a recommended pay increase of 16 cents an hour, nearly the same level all companies in all industries had been getting since the strike outbreak started in September 1945. President Truman upped the offer to 18.5 cents in lieu of working rule changes, but the unions refused. On May 23, 1946, at 4 p.m., all railroads in the United States rolled to a halt. Some researchers feel this event, more than any other, which touched every large city to every small hamlet in the country, did more than any other single event to convince the voters in the fall that something had to be done to curb the power of unions.

President Truman was furious. He called a special session of Congress and went on the air the next night to blister the railroad unions. He had taken them over under laws that were still on the books from the war, but the fact that they still walked out was the last straw. He asked the special session of Congress to give him the authority to immediately draft the strikers into military service. Then they would do as they were told or enjoy the pleasures of life in the stockade or federal prison.

Ironically, the heads of the union were negotiating in a hotel literally across the street from where Truman was speaking. During his tirade, a note was delivered on the stage saying the union had capitulated. The President asked for the new law anyhow, and was immediately given it by the house. The Senate would not go along without further discussion, and the issue was finally allowed to die a quiet legislative death. But the country greatly approved Truman's hard line.

As often happens in issues of this type, rumors were floated that once the unions heard what Truman was going to propose, they sent word they would give up the contest. But Truman wanted to give them the lashing he felt they deserved, and he went ahead, winding down only when the note appeared on the stage. Whatever the veracity of such rumors, Truman clearly made the unions an offer they couldn't refuse.

September 11, 1946—John L. Lewis made his final contribution to the election of a conservative Congress just before election day. After months of negotiations, with the government taking over the mines again on May 22, 1946, a conference was called on this date to set a day for turning the mines back to the operators now that all issues had been settled (including the by now familiar 18.5 cents per hour wage increase). The *United Mine Workers Journal* had already called the new contract, signed in President Truman's office, the best the union had ever signed in its history. The miners raised a new minor issue about how vacation payments should be made, and when the government refused to reopen the whole process over such a minor issue, especially when the new contract was concluded during the period when the government was operating the mines and thus neither side could unilaterally reopen it, Lewis claimed the contract had been breached, demanded a date for a meeting to renegotiate everything from scratch, and when refused that, he said the miners would go out on strike as of November 20, 1946. This new threat was hanging over the voters when they went to vote, and a large percentage must have found Lewis' actions increasingly aggravating based on the results of their vote.

Truman certainly found Lewis' actions troublesome. The government got a restraining order but the miners went out on strike anyhow. The government then asked the judge to find the union guilty of contempt, which the judge did. He fined the union $3.5 million, and charged Lewis personally $10,000. Lewis called off the strike on December 7 when both sides agreed to have the issue appealed directly to the Supreme Court. The Supreme Court found in the government's favor, upheld the fine against Lewis, but reduced the fine against the union to $700,000. However, this reduction was conditional. The union had to withdraw its contract termination notice, and thereby purge itself of contempt, within five days. If not, the fine automatically went back to $3.5 million. Lewis complied with the court order within the five days. He would be heard from again, but later on, especially when many union leaders considered him the "smoking gun" in the Taft-Hartley bill that the conservative Congress would pass, Lewis would find few who would listen. He was ostracized to the extent that in 1955 when the AFL and CIO reunited, Lewis was not invited to the ceremony and his name was not mentioned in the program at any point. He would be 75 years old in 1955, and would still have 14 years more to live, but as far as the labor movement was concerned, by 1955 he did not exist.

November 5, 1946—This was election day in 1946, the day the 80th Congress was elected, and the change in the Congress was remarkable. In the existing Congress, the 79th, the Senate had 57 Democrats, 36 Republicans, and one other. The Democrats had been in charge since the 1932 election, 14 years earlier. In the incoming 80th Congress, the Republicans had the lead by 51–45, a gain of 15 votes. In the existing House, in the 79th Congress, the Democrats led by 243–190 with two others. In the new 80th Congress, the Republicans led by 246–188 with one other, a gain of 56 seats for the Republicans. As in the Senate, the Democrats had been in charge since 1932 (when FDR was first elected).

This means that in 1946 the voters had thrown out the Democrats for the first time in 14 years, and they had done it in a big way. No one could have been dissatisfied with the results of World War II. The Allies had won a great victory over a truly evil enemy. What was different in 1945–46 was that the nation got to see for the first time how the unions would behave in a full employment economy with the power of the Wagner Act behind them. The people didn't like what they saw. The nation had just fought a war to rid the world of dictators, and John L. Lewis seemed to have a lot in common with many of the dictators the military had gone to so much trouble to get rid of. It seemed obvious the Wagner Act, in response to so many years of the unions being beaten down, had, as often happens, given too much to the unions. The newly elected Senators and Representatives considered themselves to have been given a mandate to restore the balance between management (at times the government, who all too often found themselves taking over the operation of manufacturing facilities) and the unions (who seemed to ignore court directives). The newly elected members of Congress set out to restore that balance.

This was not just a Republican-Democrat issue. With a Democratic president in power, whatever changes were made in the labor laws would have to override a certain presidential veto. So there would have to be some support from the other side to get a bill passed.

June 23, 1947—After almost six months of negotiations, the Congress overrode President Truman's veto of their Taft-Hartley bill (Truman had vetoed it just three days earlier). The real struggle was between the House, which basically wanted to throw the Wagner Act out and start over, and the Senate, where Bob Taft wanted to keep most of the Wagner Act and fix its deficiencies as he saw them. The House overrode the President's veto by 331–83 without even bothering to debate it again. Thus, in the House, the Republicans got a net of 85 votes other than their own (they needed a minimum of only 44 other net votes to override the veto even in the worst case). After some limited debate, the Senate overrode the veto 68–25 with two not voting. In this case, if all Senators had voted, the Republicans would have needed 13 net votes other than their own to override the veto, and they got a total of 17 with the vote as it was.

The point is that this was not just a Republican bill. Many Democratic Congressmen also felt the need to curb the power of the unions because they felt many unions had badly abused the power they had been given by the Wagner Act. Organized labor claimed it was the "Slave Labor Act" and clamored for its repeal in the next Congress that was elected in 1948. Many analysts claim this was the main thrust behind Truman's upset win in 1948. But the unions insisted on full repeal other than just some changes to parts they especially did not like (Taft was amenable to some changes), and such an "all-or-nothing" bill could not get through Congress, even though the Democrats had taken control of Congress again behind Truman's big win. The same thing happened in 1950, and the repeal of the Taft-Hartley bill became an empty campaign slogan by the time the Kennedy and Johnson Administrations came into power. The 1960s, in fact, under Lyndon Johnson, following his 1964 election, saw the passage of more "liberal" legislation than anytime since the 1930s. But the Taft-Hartley Act (and the subsequent Landrum-Griffith Act, which modified the Wagner Act further at the end of the 1950s in really a minor way—criminal activity to rip-off labor union funds was involved) were untouched.

One reason for the stability of the Taft-Hartley Act may have been revealed in the semi-memoirs of George Meany. Speaking in 1976, Meany said that labor may well have "overreacted" to the passage of the Act. He said that it now had "been on the books 29 years," and the unions still "have made progress." And they certainly haven't been "put out of business" by it. Other researchers have noted that there were rumors that labor had learned by the 1948 election that the Taft-Hartley "monster" may well have more benefits as a campaign issue than those that would accrue from its repeal. Thus, the push to repeal the act in 1948 may well have been a "phony war."

Essentially the Taft-Hartley Act retained the Wagner Act, which prohibited a whole set of actions by business. The Taft-Hartley Act then added six practices prohibited by organized labor. Meany didn't live long enough to see what many claim was the beginning of a sharp decline in labor in the 1980s (he died just as the 1980s began), or maybe his view would have been different. But as the rest of this book shows, the Taft-Hartley Act did mark a decline, however small, in labor. The power of the unions had been unchecked too long. By the time unions were professionally studying the law and planning their strategies accordingly, management was far out in front of them. The gap hasn't been closed, and, in fact, it increased greatly in the 1980s. That is why labor started its decline with the Taft-Hartley bill. It wasn't just what was in the bill, but the use that each side made of what was in the bill. Management went to work right away learning to use their brand new tools, while labor took a long time to accept that they were no longer "entitled" to an edge because of their past difficulties. This was part of the reason labor had a hard time accepting that they could no longer break the law when it seemed convenient to them. They lost the approval of the American people in the 1945–46 period, and the Taft-Hartley bill put the official seal of "no approval" on the fact. It said both sides had to follow a certain set of rules and that there were real consequences for breaking the rules. Some union members felt that the 15 years before the passage of the bill were the only chance they received to reprimand management for previous wrong treatment.

December 12, 1947—John L. Lewis took a big step backwards from what little standing he had left in the labor community. Lewis and his coal miners had reaffiliated with the AFL in 1946 after Lewis' dramatic withdrawal from being President of the CIO and his subsequent takeover of the Presidency of the coal miner union once again. Lewis was looking for a cause to support and the passage of the Taft-Hartley bill with its requirement for an anti-communist "loyalty oath" gave him just that. But George Meany, only the second man in the AFL as its Secretary-Treasurer, was taking more and more responsibility in the AFL as President William Green (now 75 years old with only five more years to live), was growing ever more fragile.

Lewis wanted to "boycott" the Taft-Hartley Act by having everyone refuse to sign the oath. But any union refusing to sign lost the protections offered by the National Labor Relations Board (NLRB), which essentially meant they lost the protections of the Wagner Act while still being subject to the new punishments of the Taft-Hartley Act. Lewis came to a pre-convention AFL Executive Council meeting to present his side, but Meany stood up and challenged him. Lewis and Meany had never had any previous interchanges, and Lewis dismissed him as not being in charge of an individual union. This began a conflict.

At the AFL convention in San Francisco in November 1947, prepared addresses to the convention were to be read. Lewis attacked once more, first explaining that everyone knew he was not a communist, and how he threw them out of his coal miners union. However, he had admitted communists in 1935. Lewis condemned the AFL leadership, specifically President William Green, as being a collection of "lions led by asses." In fact, he corrected himself, the AFL didn't have a head on the Taft-Hartley affidavit issue, "its neck has just grown up and haired over." It was vintage Lewis.

Meany responded that the Taft-Hartley Act was now the law of the land as enacted through the democratic process of the United States, and the "only way it is going to be changed is through our representatives under our system." So much for Lewis' "boycott." As for the affidavit, Meany saw no reason to "pull the communist chestnuts out of the fire." Their objective has been "the destruction of the AFL.... In 1935 they found a national home. They went into the CIO. They are still there today." He reminded Lewis that Lewis was the one who admitted communists into the coal miners' union before passing leadership to Phil Murray. He told Lewis that Lewis waved anti-communism banners for his miners union with his right hand, but gave his left hand in fellowship to a long list of now-known communists in the CIO. Meany stated that he personally was quite willing to sign the affidavit, and for that matter, was willing to sign another affidavit the he, Meany, was "never a comrade to the comrades."

Lewis and most of the other delegates were stunned. No one had ever confronted Lewis in that matter. As a final touch, the AFL replaced Lewis on the Executive Committee and Lewis did not even bother to run for election to his position. He knew it was all over. A few weeks later a friend of Lewis' daughter, Kathryn, who supposedly had some influence over him, sent a message to Meany (Lewis now realized who was the real power in the AFL) that he, Lewis, would not withdraw from the AFL again, as was rumored, if the AFL would make some public gesture that they wanted him to stay. But Meany was now another person for whom Lewis' antics were troublesome. To the emissary, who was a man, Meany said his response was to tell Lewis to "go to hell."

On December 12, 1947, the date at the heading of this entry, Lewis sent a note that said simply: "Green: We disaffiliate. Lewis." Green was of course still the official AFL President and was the only official who could act on such a note. The Mine Workers Union was once again an independent union, outside both the AFL and CIO. Lewis retired as president of the union in 1960 at the age of 80, and when he died at 89 in 1969, they were still an independent union. Meany never relented. The coal miners' union is still outside today, a shadow of its former self, with oil and natural gas taking over its prime heating functions. It can be said that John L. Lewis' biggest enemy was himself.

November 5, 1949—At the CIO convention two unions were expelled for being under the control of communists, and, on this specific date, charges were brought against 10 other affiliated unions. Investigations were ordered, and most of these unions were expelled in 1950. The net loss to the CIO was 11 unions, as one union was able to throw out the communists who held positions on its board on its own and stay affiliated. This was the culmination of a long process dating back to the 1948 election battle between the CIO followers of Henry Wallace (seen as a communist dupe by most observers) and the 1947 Taft-Hartley battle over the signing of the non-communist affidavit.

Most of the credit has to be given to President Phil Murray, who stated that communist-controlled unions could no longer be tolerated in the CIO. Under his leadership the convention introduced a resolution that "we can no longer tolerate within the family of the CIO the Communist party masquerading as a labor union." This was in line with new CIO policies that had been developed to keep communists from controlling any unions affiliated with the CIO. The CIO constitution was amended to specifically bar any officers or members of the Executive Boards from being communists or fascists.

Although not much was made of it then, the removal of the communist-controlled unions from the CIO would play a big part in the reunion of the AFL and the CIO in 1955.

May 23, 1950—On this date, GM and Walter Reuther of the United Auto Workers (UAW) reached an agreement on an historic contract. GM continued the cost-of living adjustments (COLA) that had been a revolutionary feature of the two-year contract reached on May 25, 1948. The fact that the prior contract was two years in length was also a new feature. Reuther, just out of the hospital after an assassination attempt in 1948, found Chares E. Wilson, a GM executive with vision and brutal honesty, an executive he could deal with, because he felt Wilson was much like himself. It didn't hurt that GM, with 45 percent of the domestic market and no foreign rivals, was making a phenomenal return on assets.

In 1950, the two men took another step. GM offered more improvements in every phase of the contract in exchange for a contract length of five years. In what was called the "Treaty of Detroit," each side got something they wanted—with no strike. It was pointed out by Fortune magazine that GM may have paid literally a billion dollars for labor peace, but GM had learned from the longer 1948 contract that knowing there will be no production halts due to strikes made it possible to plan carefully for model changes, and tool and plant investment. The other car companies (and companies in other industries) ended up following the GM model. Nearly every company wished they had thought before about longer contracts because the common complaint was that after the tensions of hammering out this year's deal, it was already time to think about changes for next year.

Reuther was a new star in the newspapers, and predictions were made about his making a possible run for the presidency. But that prediction had also been made back in the 1940s when President Truman told President Phil Murray of the CIO that the "young red-headed engineer" (which is what Roosevelt thought Reuther was after he made a number of recommendations in a series of meetings for increasing war production), was after Murray's job. Murray replied with a smile, "No, Mr. President, he's after your job." Eleanor Roosevelt took Walter Reuther as a protégé, and opened a lot of doors for him in Washington. It took a lot of pressure from Reuther's family (often derisively called "The Royal Family" by Reuther's opponents) to keep him actively pursuing the union business, the purest calling his father could imagine. Reuther specifically was kept on the union track by being told that he would have to start all over at the bottom in the race for the UAW presidency if he took even a temporary Washington detour, and that convinced him to stay focused on Detroit. It was the UAW presidency he wanted above all.

Reuther was certainly ambitious. He was born on Labor Day eve in 1907 as the youngest of four sons (much later a fifth child, a girl, arrived) to Valentine Reuther, a German immigrant who was a pure socialist and unionist. Walter was part of discussions around the dinner table as soon as he could join in about how socialism would solve the world's problems if only unions and others could spread the word. Walter and his brother Victor actually spent nearly three years in Russia helping to teach tool and die-making to workers there, returning to Detroit just in time in 1935 to take part in the formation of what eventually became the United Auto Workers (UAW). He was one victim of the infamous "battle of the overpass" on May 26, 1937, when some Ford goons beat him and three other organizers who were standing on an overpass at a Ford Plant trying to hand out leaflets as part of an organizing drive. Among other things, Walter was thrown down two flights of cement steps.

He persevered. Walter Reuther was elected President of the UAW by a very narrow margin over the "communist bloc" in 1946, and then put himself firmly in control in 1947 (when he invited his father Valentine to attend and give a rousing pro-union speech to a standing ovation). Reuther threw out the communists who had wanted to control the UAW, and he converted many opponents to his side by permitting them to stay in low-level positions in the union management chain rather than having to return to jobs on the factory floor at a relatively advanced age. Most had made their career as union officers and were in no shape to actually work on a production line again. They were suitably grateful and formed a core of support for Reuther.

Reuther remained president of the UAW until he was killed in an airplane crash in 1970; never giving up the job even when he was elected president of the CIO after Phil Murray died in 1952. Reuther became famous in union history by leading (and winning) the fight for such now generally accepted things as COLAs and wage increases based on productivity gains, longer term contracts, a guaranteed annual wage, improved pension benefits, a stock sharing plan for union members, and many retirement and health-related benefits that later were copied in many other negotiations in other industries that never dreamed of such union gains.

Reuther was one of the giant figures in the history of labor. He was much like John L. Lewis in constantly coming up with new innovations and delivering the goods for his union members. But he was also much like Lewis in his need to be the leader or nothing. He helped bring the AFL and CIO back together in 1955, but he finally pulled the UAW out of the combination in the next decade, primarily because he preferred to have things done his own way.

November 9, 1952—On this date, Phil Murray, president of the CIO since John L. Lewis resigned at the end of 1940, died at the age of 66. A dozen days later, on November 21, 1952, William Green, president of the AFL who had been in failing health for some time, died at the age of 79. Green had replaced Samuel Gompers as head of the AFL in 1924. Thus, Green was the last direct contact to what we now consider the beginning of organized labor in the United States when Gompers formed the AFL in 1886, although at the time of Green's death Secretary-Treasurer George Meany was effectively running the AFL because of the poor health of Green.

Ironically, the death of the two famous leaders, essentially at the same time, opened the door for the reunification of the AFL and the CIO. Negotiations (or at least many letters and memos) for reunification between the two federations, with Presidents Roosevelt and Truman in the mix, as well as the ever-present John L. Lewis, had been going on for more than a decade, but no basis had been reached to set up even one serious meeting to address the subject. One problem, of course, was the personalities of the men involved. All had problems considering working for one of the others in a combined organization. This was in spite of, or maybe even due to, the fact that the men involved had been working together for decades in most cases. But now two of them were dead, Lewis was still making mischief but was no longer regarded a serious candidate by labor in general, and with new men taking over the AFL and CIO, a new opportunity for reunification was suddenly at hand.

November 25, 1952—According to Meany, his election to become the new president of the AFL was settled on the morning of this date, the same day as the funeral of William Green. The Executive Council voted 7–6 to install Meany rather than Bill Tobin, another long-time toiler in the vineyards of the AFL who had also requested the opportunity to do the job, at least for a year or two. Meany held the job for 27 years until the end of 1979 when poor health forced him to nominate Lane Kirkland for the job at the AFL convention held near the end of 1979. Meany was wheeled away in his wheelchair after Kirkland was unanimously elected. Meany died eight weeks later on January 10, 1980, at the age of 86. The fact that Meany did not retire at a "reasonable" age was one of the reasons Reuther finally took his UAW out of the combined AFL-CIO in 1968.

Walter Reuther also had one serious contender, Allan S. Haywood, to replace William Murray as head of the CIO. Haywood was nominated by David J. McDonald, who, as head of the steel workers union, had been a long time opponent of Reuther. The final vote was 3,078,181 for Reuther compared to 2,613,103 for Haywood. If Meany's story is true, he had only 53.8 percent of his total vote while Reuther had 54.1 percent of his total vote. Certainly neither man was an overwhelming choice, but by the end of 1952 both federations had new leaders, and both professed to be in favor of reunification.

April 7, 1953—The first unity meeting was held by a committee with members from both the AFL and the CIO to discuss what both sides saw as a major obstacle to reunification—the question of "raiding" each other's unions for new members. A study of the previous two years showed that of the 1,246 bargaining elections that could be defined as "raids," only about 17 percent of the workers voted to change unions. Further, the net shift between the two federations was about 7,000 of the 366,470 workers involved in the elections. Raiding was suddenly recognized as a perceived, but not real, problem. By June 2, 1953, a no-raiding agreement had been hammered out, and it was approved at the December conventions of each federation and signed by both chief officers on December 16, 1953. It would be tried on a trial basis for two years. There were further discussions, but a final agreement was signed on June 9, 1954. Reunification was one step closer.

February 8, 1955—One final issue, the question of jurisdiction, i.e., who would be in charge in cases where AFL and CIO unions were both affiliated with similar unions (nearly the old "dual union" issue) was resolved by following Meany's suggestion that they merge and solve such issues as they arose rather than trying to solve them all first, because that would take forever. The new constitution would state "both craft and industrial unions are appropriate, equal, and necessary as methods of trade union organization." A merger agreement was signed on this date by a joint committee in Miami, a constitution was drafted in Washington on May 2, 1955, and after parallel conventions were held in New York on December 1, 1955, a joint convention of the newly merged federation would be held on December 5, 1955. At that time, reunification would be a fact. The name of the merged operation would be the American Federation of Labor—Congress of Industrial Organizations.

December 5, 1955—This was the first official convention of the merged organization. George Meany was the designated president of the merged organization because the AFL had about twice as many members as the CIO at the time of the merger (the combined federation had 15 million members, making it the largest union anywhere in the free world. The CIO had an estimated total of 4–6 million, depending whose numbers were used. It probably did not contain more than five million, giving the AFL a true 2:1 advantage or more). Meany had assumed the CIO would take the next most powerful position, Secretary-Treasurer, and he had even prepared a new position within the AFL for his existing Secretary-Treasurer, Bill Schnitzler, to move into after the merger. But much to everyone's surprise, Walter Reuther declined the position, and even more, declined to appoint anyone from the CIO to fill it. So the AFL took the two highest ranking positions at his urging.

The rumor from the CIO side was that Reuther did not want anyone to outrank him in the old CIO organization, which the combined secretary-treasurer position would do. Reuther did not want to leave his spot as President of his beloved UAW, meaning he did not want the secretary-treasurer job himself, but he did not want anyone else from the old CIO to have it either. So he just let the AFL side keep it. It was reasonable for Reuther to hope, at the age of 48 in 1955 at the time of the merger, that Meany, who was 61 at the time of the merger, would retire in a small number of years and give Reuther a crack at the top job. But Meany had joked more than once that he planned to die while still in office, and anyone who knew Meany well knew it was no joke.

But Reuther was not meant to be number two. It was another of the personality quirks that Reuther shared with John L. Lewis, one that did them both a disservice. The only role Reuther wanted was that of leader, and there was only room for one leader on a team. Both men were also similar in that they loved their jobs as president of their specific unions, and they were uncommonly good at it. Their members benefited greatly from the expertise of the big guy at the top. But no matter how good they were at the "nuts and bolts" union level, both had higher ambitions.

As noted before, the merger effectively ended the career of Lewis. He made several written commendations during the negotiations, especially to his old CIO contacts, but no one carried them forward. They knew no one would trust any recommendations from Lewis, no matter how useful they might seem, because everyone would assume they carried a hidden agenda. Lewis himself did not attend any sessions, and as his union was not affiliated with either side at the time (it is still listed as an independent union). Neither he nor his union was part of the conventions held in December, the last on December first for both the AFL and CIO as separate federations, and the first on December fifth for the AFL-CIO as a combined federation. Lewis was not mentioned in any official way at the merger convention—and any unofficial mentions he may have gathered were certainly not favorable. The founder of the CIO had ceased to exist.

It could be argued that Reuther's career ended at this convention. There were a few more famous negotiations he was given credit for, including Ford's acceptance of the Supplemental Unemployment Benefit (SUB) in 1955 as a way of delivering a guaranteed annual wage. Ford was the target of this negotiation because after Charles Wilson left GM, Reuther found GM management much more rigid. So when he wanted new ideas, he went to Ford, but when he wanted cash he went to GM. However, as the 1950s, ended foreign car competition appeared in the United States from Germany and Japan, and the great cash flow in Detroit began to subside. Other persons appeared on the UAW negotiating teams as Reuther focused on other areas, but no matter how well trained they were they didn't have the Reuther touch for the limited sums available.

The other problem was that Reuther turned his attention to what he called "the social contract" he believed unions had with the American people. He tried to use the UAW as a vehicle for social change, and he found that, as Sam Gompers had preached for years, union members were interested in the here and now, not "pie in the sky." Reuther became deeply involved with the Democratic Party, and then, when it failed to meet his vision, he undertook to change it. Reuther never could understand why others were not as interested in "political progress" as he was, when, after all, he only had their best interests in mind. Reuther lost his edge for "strictly" union work after the merger, and if he had gotten the chance to run the AFL-CIO in place of Meany after the 1950s, it's unlikely he would have done as good a job for the members as Meany did. Reuther was never as great a "grass roots" labor champion after the merger as he was before, and his refusal to be Secretary-Treasurer was one of the reasons.

John L. Lewis retired from the presidency of his coal miners in 1960 at the age of 80, and he died in virtual obscurity in 1969 at the age of 89. Reuther died one year later in a plane crash, at the age of 63 in 1970, and Meany died at 86 in January of 1980 (after finally giving up his presidency eight weeks earlier in December of 1979). Both Reuther and Meany received sumptuous funerals and all the "usual" high-level "suspects" attended the funerals of both men at the time, but it really was the "old-time" labor movement that was interred for good when these three men died. The unionized labor movement held relatively steady after the merger, falling from 35.5 percent of the total labor force in 1945 to 33.2 percent by the merger in 1955 (staying above 30 percent in the other years in spite of the communist-directed unions that had been expelled); and holding in at 31.4 percent in 1960. But by 1965 it was down to 28.4 percent, and it has fallen steadily to its present level of 13.5 percent (including many new governmental unions that did not exist when it peaked back in 1945). The rest of this chronology describes its persistent (and probably inevitable) decline.

September 14, 1959—President Eisenhower on this date signed the Labor-Management Reporting and Disclosure Act, which became known as the Landrum-Griffith Act after Democratic Representative Phil Landrum of Georgia and Republican Representative Robert Griffith of Michigan, the two sponsors of the Act. Part of it was an outgrowth of the famous McClelland Committee hearings that began in 1957 on corruption in Labor unions. Senator John L. McClelland nearly became a famous TV star because of these hearings, and the extensive 1960 presidential race coverage of Kennedy versus Nixon owes a debt to these hearings as politicians saw the impact television coverage had on the nation.

Watching Teamsters President Dave Beck sitting before the committee taking the Fifth Amendment on each and every question easily convinced the public that the unions had plenty to hide. The fact that the AFL-CIO, pushed by Meany, had kicked out the Teamsters, the Bakery and Confectionery, and Laundry Workers unions in 1957 as a result of investigations the AFL-CIO had started earlier on their own made little difference, even among the few who knew what the federation was and what they had done. The television verdict was that union officials were a bunch of crooks who stole from their members.

Attempts had been ongoing by both sides to modify the Taft-Hartley Act (the idea of "repeal" had long since been discarded), and the Landrum-Griffin Act was the ideal opportunity. Nobody was really opposed to the sections addressing the corruption that had been uncovered (except the union officials themselves), but both labor and management saw a chance to change either the Taft-Hartley Act and/or parts of the original Wagner Act that the Taft-Hartley Act left unchanged. A bill more favorable to labor passed the Senate 90–1, but in the house the much tougher Landrum-Griffith bill passed 229–201 (even though the Democrats held an edge of 283–153 in the house and 64–34 in the Senate). It was softened a little towards labor in a conference committee, and then sent to Eisenhower. He signed the bill on September 14, the date of this entry.

Once again, this should have been a big warning signal to labor. The recession of 1958 gave the Democrats an edge in the 1958 Congressional elections, and thus a big edge in the 1959–60 Congress, but labor admitted it lost on the Landrum-Griffith law. The nation had been turned off on unions by the McClelland hearings. Union membership fell to 31.4 percent of the workforce in 1960, back to where it was in the early 1940s.

November 22, 1963—This date is infamous as the day on which President Kennedy was assassinated, but it was also the first day of President Lyndon Johnson's first term. With good times in the country and the sympathy factor still resounding from the events of 1963, Johnson won a record-breaking election on his own on November 3, 1964. Given his announcement in early 1968 that he would not run again so that he could concentrate on efforts to achieve peace in Vietnam, Johnson had just a little over five full years in the White House (Kennedy had just under three years in the White House).

Johnson oversaw the passage of more "liberal" legislation in those four years than any president before or since except President Franklin D. Roosevelt. Johnson looked like an average American, but with his eight years of experience as the Senate Majority and Minority leader in the 1950s, and a total of 23 years in the Congress starting in 1937, he knew more about the legislative process than perhaps anybody who ever served in that body. His "aw, shucks" manner notwithstanding, his was nobody's fool, but his determination to have "guns and butter" in pursuing the Vietnam mess left a permanent stain on his administration.

Elected with an overwhelming Congressional majority of 68–32 in the Senate and 295–140 in the house, Johnson was determined to complete all the "liberal" legislation Kennedy had wanted to pass (Kennedy was unable to pass anything in his brief time on the job), and Johnson also added much more. This had a quite unintended effect on the future growth of unions, even though they all applauded the Johnson legislative effort. Johnson could count major civil rights, anti-poverty, aid to education, minimum-wage increases, fair housing, and health-care bills (including Medicare and Medicaid) among his accomplishments—his whole "Great Society" Program.

From another point of view, he accomplished many of the things unions said were their goals for many years. His accomplishments raised the question of why laborers would join unions. If a laborer carefully considered all the protections afforded him through Federal and State statutes, and he was a skilled craftsman whose talents were in demand, he would have to justify carefully in his own mind why he should give a union any money. If a downturn came and he had to go out looking for a new job and needed support in the form of cash in the meantime, it's local state and federal agencies he'll be dealing with, not the union. Reuther used to push for the "union welfare state," but it appears Lyndon Johnson did it for him.

It should also be noted that with his "veto proof" majorities, Johnson and the Democrats were unable to change either the Wagner Act, the Taft-Hartley Act, or the Landrum-Griffith Act. They tried to change the section dealing with union-shop contracts, but were unable to stop a Senate filibuster led by minority leader Everett Dirksen, in spite of the extent by which the Republicans were outnumbered. There could have been many reasons why no bills were passed in these areas, but one reason could have been that the Federal Government was satisfied that labor and management were close enough to an equal playing field and the Acts should be left alone. It might also have been that, as in 1946, after labor had finished its 1945–46 strike run, there was no public support to specifically help unions. Also, after everyone had had a chance to watch the McClelland hearings (aided by special counsel Robert Kennedy) that showed how corruption had spread through the organized labor movement, the public opinion of unions was lowered. All of the many famous "liberal" bills passed by the Johnson Administration delivered their benefits directly to the people. No union was needed to intercede. Although much less publicity attended similar bills passed by subsequent Democratic (or Republican for that matter) administrations, the key is that the benefits generally went directly to the people. Union help was generally not mandatory. This was another trend that reduced the need for a worker to join a union.

July 1, 1968—This was the date that Walter Reuther formally took his United Auto Workers (UAW) out of the AFL-CIO. It was the culmination of a personal struggle between Reuther and George Meany that had gone on since 1955, but which reached a peak for at least the last two years. But it must be said that most of the struggle was on the side of Reuther. Meany thought Reuther was behaving in an almost irrational way, especially in the later 1960s, and he seemed not to care strongly what Reuther did or did not do. Meany was busy supporting in Congress the great legislative output being presided over by Lyndon Johnson.

Some claim the generally poor relations between Meany and Reuther came to a head in 1966 when Meany went into the hospital for major hip surgery at the age of 71. Meany was in the hospital for a month, and then underwent arduous rehabilitation exercises for six months. He went from a wheelchair to canes to walking freely again, and looked younger than ever. This seemed to be the final proof that Meany intended to die in his position, and that his death was still far in the future. The realization that Reuther was a long time from succeeding Meany seemed to be the trigger for a series of almost irrational moves by Reuther that led to his withdrawal on this date.

It was no secret that Reuther wanted to replace Meany. After Reuther's withdrawal Meany would quip that the "only anti-Reuther thing I did in my lifetime was to preserve my health." Meany had also been heard to say that the only thing he could do to please Reuther was to drop dead. The men had completely different personalities, and completely different ideas on how to advance the cause of labor. Reuther was rather ascetic, and one of his pet peeves was that Meany would hold the AFL-CIO conventions in the palatial hotels in Miami Beach. Once a reporter asked a group of leaders at the convention where Reuther was when the reporter noticed Reuther was not among the group having a good time in a beautifully appointed conference room, and he was jokingly told that Reuther was down the hall in a linen closet squeezing his own orange juice.

About the only similarity between the two men was their integrity. It was unquestioned in both, and both were men of their word. This was one of the things that disturbed Meany the most as their relationship went sour, because Reuther would often refuse to come to AFL-CIO headquarters to discuss apparent problems stating he was "too busy." Meany might solve (in his mind) an issue by telling someone "go to hell," while Reuther might actually tell someone the same thing, but he would do it in a speech that ran for over an hour. Reuther performed with excellence and poise on the stump, while Meany went straight to the heart of the issue as he saw it.

Reuther was also in the middle of a crisis in the UAW at the time (a reporter noted that the UAW was "a union in search of a mission"). The explosion of militant blacks in the 1960s not only led to the Detroit riots of

1967, but along with all the other groups marching against the Vietnam War, led to an influx of new union members who didn't believe in taking orders from anyone, and who would readily resort to sabotage to get their way with management regardless of what the union contract said (even assuming they could or would read it). They had no knowledge of what it took to get the UAW to its present status, and they didn't want to know. In 1968 a black organization known as the Dodge Revolutionary Union Movement (DRUM) insisted that Reuther and half of the UAW top positions be replaced with blacks. One of their leaflets urged "Behead the Redhead." Reuther was upset at the nonsensical "militants" shouting for attention in a way that ignored all he had done for the UAW in bringing blacks into the union in the past, whereas someone like Meany would have simply shrugged and said that it has to be accepted that no good deed ever goes unpunished.

But Reuther was truly looking for a mission. Once he left the AFL-CIO (he was surprised to find no other union left with him), he tried to form an alliance with the outcast Teamsters union. In 1967 Jimmy Hoffa had entered Lewisburg Federal Prison to begin serving an eight-year sentence for jury tampering. His handpicked replacement, Frank Fitzsimmons, had surprised many by trying to be more than just a caretaker for the union. He had moved the union to the left regarding Vietnam (Hoffa had nothing but disdain for such issues), and Fitzsimmons impressed Reuther by being one of the few high level union officials to attend Martin Luther King's funeral in the spring of 1968.

Reuther and Fitzsimmons represented two of the biggest unions in the United States, and combined they had the resources to implement far-reaching programs even if they both were now outside the mainstream. Reuther had begun preliminary discussions about what came to be called the Alliance for Labor Action (ALA) even before he formally left the AFL-CIO. With a total of more of three and a half million dues paying members, the ALA was bigger and richer than the CIO was at its founding in 1935, and even in this era the two unions were about one-quarter the size of the present AFL-CIO. The two men agreed that the Teamsters would focus on recruiting and organizing new members, while the UAW would concentrate on community and social action projects that were Reuther's specialty.

But the ALA was like oil and water. The Teamster officials below the top level were anxious to add new members, but they looked on Reuther's projects as just another philanthropic group like the Ford Foundation (which in fact did take over one of Reuther's projects after the UAW spun it off in early 1969). What Reuther was missing was "radical" young people with "stars in their eyes," not unlike his former self. Many such "radical" people were already in the UAW, but they were interested in "more and more right here and now," not something like Reuther's Citizens Crusade Against Poverty, which the Ford Foundation would later absorb. The black militants were operating in the new UAW, and their interest was taking charge, as soon as they could take it. By 1970 they would account for almost one-quarter of all autoworkers in the Detroit area, and they saw Reuther as seriously out of touch. "Put Walter in a Halter" was one of the milder slogans. Reuther decided serious education for union members was needed to make them understand where the union had come from and where it should be going. He knew his days as UAW president were numbered (mandatory retirement was only four years away in 1969 when he turned 62). He had been working on an UAW education center at the Black Lake resort area about 260 miles north of Detroit where union members would learn how to be union members in the Reuther mode while also enjoying a first-class vacation. He hoped to run the operation and do some teaching there when he retired. Like much of the last years of his life, it was a plan he would not realize.

May 9, 1970—On a private jet flight to check some last minute details at Black Lake, which was due to be dedicated in June, Walter Reuther, his wife May, the Black Lake architect, and Reuther's nephew, who was also his bodyguard, were killed with the two pilots when the Lear Jet crashed in a huge fireball while trying to land at Black Lake. Of the six towering figures of organized labor in the United States, five (Samuel Gompers, William Green, Phil Murray, John L. Lewis, and Walter Reuther) were now dead, and George Meany was the only one still active. He would be gone in another decade.

Reuther died at the end of the boom years following World War II, and possibly at the peak of the civil unrest of the 1960s and 1970s (four students at Kent State were shot and killed five days before Reuther's plane crashed during a demonstration). The boom went bust with the 1974 oil crisis, as cheap high-mileage Japanese cars won one-quarter of the national automobile market during the decade. In the meantime, non-union labor manufacturing plants were enjoying great success in Alabama, Tennessee, and other sunbelt states. Chrysler was saved from bankruptcy in 1979 only by a controversial federal loan that required the UAW to cut wages and benefits.

This led to a number of management "copycat" efforts to reduce wages and close plants. Between 1970 and 1980, union membership stayed nearly constant at 19.6 million, but as a percentage of the workforce, it fell from 27.3 percent in 1970 to 21.9 percent in 1980, a decrease of almost exactly 20 percent for the decade. It was the beginning of what many present union members feared would be the end.

November 7, 1972—Richard Nixon was reelected President of the United States in an historical landslide. This election left Congress firmly in the hands of the Democrats, but was a personal triumph for Nixon. It also ratified the split that was taking place in organized labor. The militants, black and white, who had been pouring into the labor unions since the later 1960s, were not welcomed by the older members. They had a lot of words for each other, but "solidarity" was not one of them. The Teamsters endorsed Nixon in the 1972 election, perhaps the closing act for the Alliance for Labor Action between the Teamsters and the UAW, which was destined to wither away after Reuther's death.

A sharp recession began in late 1974, and by January of 1975 unemployment was at rates not seen since the depression (Nixon was gone by now due to the Watergate Scandal). Nearly one-quarter of all UAW members were on indefinite layoff, and the militants, in the sense of last hired-first fired, were gone from the plants (some with the help of the union if seniority didn't get rid of those wished gone). This was the final result of the ugly campaign of 1968, in which George Wallace helped Nixon beat Hubert Humphrey while hard-hat construction workers fought with Vietnam protesters in the streets of New York. Similar things happened in 1972.

George Meany of the AFL-CIO bumped heads with Nixon on almost everything, but he once stated that if Nixon was the number one anticommunist in the states, he, Meany, was surely number two. Meany finally turned against Nixon when all the details of the Watergate cover-up came out, and Meany called for Nixon's resignation. But otherwise Meany supported Nixon's foreign policy as long as it took a hard anti-communist line and stayed away from calling for detente. So in this part of the 1970s we had the unions supporting the elimination of the militants from unions nationwide, and supporting a very hard line overseas. Reuther was already considered part of another time and another place.

November 2, 1976—The election of Jimmy Carter on this date (by the closest electoral vote in 60 years) is significant for labor in the sense that Carter only spent four years in office, losing to Ronald Reagan in 1980. The things that happened in the Reagan Administration practically put organized labor out of business, or, as many say today, made it irrelevant to the nation's economy.

Carter actually won the election in 1974 when then president Gerald Ford pardoned Richard Nixon, who had resigned due to the Watergate scandal. Such a pardon was part of a deal that was to have resulted in a long-sought Nixon confession, but his subsequent "confession" was very vague. This pardon may have led to Ford's loss of the next election.

Carter beat Ford by a narrow margin. Carter carried a good Democratic margin in both the house and senate, with much campaigning by blacks in general and the AFL-CIO specifically, and organized labor had high hopes for some favorable legislation, with a jobs program at the head of the list.

But it was not to be. Carter could not get legislation favorable to labor through the Congress.

In early 1979, George Meany was asked at a press conference if he had a candidate he would prefer to see at the top of the Democratic ticket for president in 1980 (Carter was already being tossed aside in many people's minds), Meany said "Yes, Harry Truman. I wish he was here." But Meany would not be alive to see the 1980 presidential campaign. He was 85 years old in 1979, and his wife died in March at the age of 82, following a long illness and a marriage of 60 years. Meany was crushed by her death, and he was never the same afterwards. He was soon confined to a wheelchair due to a knee problem, and that is how he presided over his last AFL-CIO convention in November 1979, when he nominated Lane Kirkland to succeed him and watched as Kirkland was unanimously elected. But the big news that November was the seizing of the United States Embassy in Iran and the taking of the hostages there. It was what would become the final blow for the Carter Administration.

January 14, 1980—Meany died in January at 86, and on this date a poignant photo was taken of an union member in overalls and work clothes paying his last respects at AFL-CIO headquarters in Washington, as he holds his work hat crushed in his hand and looks into Meany's open coffin. It had far more impact than all the pictures that followed of the usual crowd of top dignitaries at Meany's funeral at St. Matthew's Cathedral in Washington. The union member was looking at the passing of more than just an era.

Meany was the last of the six towering figures of organized labor in the United States to pass from the scene. Samuel Gompers, William Green, and Meany carried the AFL forward for almost exactly a century, and John L. Lewis, Phil Murray, and Walter Reuther carried the CIO forward from its break out of the AFL in 1935 to its reunification with the AFL in 1955, with Reuther taking tentative steps towards another break when he died in 1970. Everything that took place to move organized labor in the United States to its peak between 1935 and 1945 happened while one or more of these men was active in the movement, except, of course, Samuel Gompers. And it's easy to mark 1980 as the end of the six men and the beginning of the end of organized labor as a relevant part of the economic scene in the United States.

Organized labor as a relevant factor started in 1935, peaked in 1945, held its own until 1955, slid slowly sideways and downward in 1965, slid a little further down by 1975, and then fell into submission as the 1980s opened.

November 4, 1980—Ronald Reagan was elected president in an unexpectedly large landslide over Carter. The reasons were many. Reagan brought enough Republican Senators with him for the Republicans to gain control of the Senate for the first time since 1952, when Dwight Eisenhower was elected president for his first term. The Democrats maintained control of the house 242–192, even though they lost 35 seats, and in large portions of the South it was hard to separate Democrats from Republicans in terms of their political inclinations, regardless of what nametag they wore on their lapels.

It was not a favorable outlook for organized labor, and they did not get much from Jimmy Carter, who turned out to be much more conservative than they expected any Democrat to be. Then Reagan turned out to be even tougher than labor could have imagined.

August 5, 1981—If one needed a specific date when organized labor began its free fall over the precipice, this is it. This is the date President Reagan fired unconditionally the air traffic controllers who refused to come back to work. And he made it stick.

Two days earlier the Professional Air Traffic Controllers Organization (PATCO) went on strike. They knew it was illegal, as are all such strikes by federal or state employees, employees that play a critical role in the ongoing business and/or education of the nation. But they considered also the strike by the postal workers on March 17, 1970, which was just as illegal. It ran for about one week, even with federal and state troops (the National Guard) being called in to sort the mail. At one point a federal worker from another union suggested they all go out on strike after watching the postal workers for a few days, because, as he was quoted in the Washington Post, "they can't fire all of us." This was the essence of nearly all illegal "wildcat" strikes. The unions knew they were illegal, but unions had been thumbing their noses at laws they didn't like and they felt couldn't be enforced since they took a no-strike pledge during World War II, which they broke literally thousands of times. The union leaders simply threw up their hands and said they didn't authorize the strikes and thus they were not liable. Even after Taft-Hartley, unions often felt they were above the law because they "deserved" whatever it was they illegally struck for.

It is truly impossible to over-emphasize how Reagan's actions changed the relationship in disputes between labor and management. The PATCO union president misled his union about the non-actions the government would take. He stated that the issues, which had been ongoing for a long time and had come to a head, were ignored by the Carter administration and they were going on strike whether Reagan liked it or not. Reagan told them instantly that their actions were illegal, and they in essence had one day (and months and months of dragging appeals through the courts) to decide to stop the strike or be fired. They would be permanently replaced, and they would not be rehired until far into the future, if they were ever rehired, based on their taking part in the illegal strike (it would be a decade before one of the strikers would be rehired by the then new controller's union). The union ignored Reagan's threats and continued the strike.

The union (and the rest of the labor movement) received a shock when Reagan fired all of the controllers immediately. He then set to work bringing in supervisors, military controllers, and accelerating the controllers training program to move those near the top into control towers everywhere. With some flight adjustments worked out with the airlines, the whole thing went off without a hitch. Soon nobody noticed that the original controllers were gone. As almost always happens in such situations, the FAA found out they needed far fewer controllers than they had been operating with, and they lowered the number of new controllers needed to get back to "full strength." People lined up to enter the training programs for what were very well paying jobs in spite of the union claims of "terrible stress," and it was as if nothing had ever happened. There were no problems.

But something major had happened. First of all, the PATCO workers had been lied to. They had been assured Reagan didn't have the guts to fire them, and, even if he did, they would certainly be aided by the public outcry and other unions. The public "outcry" became a standing ovation because the public had grown tried of anything militant by the end of the 1970s. The AFL-CIO followed their legal advice not to become involved. Even the machinists union, which could most affect the issue by taking action against the flight schedule of the planes, held off, as their president said he had been told by their attorneys that "if he should sanction, encourage, or approve a sympathy strike under these conditions," he would risk the entire financial reserves of his union. Essentially PATCO received little support.

The experience of PATCO ran through the minds of future unions when they were being encouraged by both management and union officials alike to vote one way or another in an upcoming election. Their union officials had trained them not to believe anything management told them, but the new voters had to wonder if the PATCO president hadn't shown that union leaders could not be trusted.

In addition, the PATCO affair was the impetus for a movement that had begun to blossom in the 1970s. Management consulting firms were formed to tell companies how to legally get rid of, or greatly diminish the negative effects of, unions. After all, there were only three basic acts affecting management and labor relationships—the Wager Act of 1935, the Taft-Hartley Act of 1947, and the Landrum-Griffith Act of 1959. A careful reading of each act may prove more fruitful than noisy public marches that disrupt traffic and turn public opinion on the side of management. Hiring a group of lawyers (or consultants) knowledgeable about these acts could provide a very useful investment. The unions seemed to be willing to use their old techniques from the past, legal or illegal. Reagan had shown them the power of standing up to these tactics if one had the law on his side and was prepared to act decisively. Appendix A shows how dramatically strikes fell off after 1980, suggesting that the unions were soon taught by management and their consultants that the old way didn't work anymore. The three key acts were now quite old, and any clever lawyer or consultant should be able to show how some new techniques would work better in today's world than the union's old approach of counting on noisy, messy strikes and hoping for some new laws from a pliable Congress.

This is a good point to once again use a comparison of the incredibly complicated tax code with the labor laws and their cousins known as the employment laws (minimum wage, health, safety, racial and gender discrimination, etc.). An income tax expert for the government once pointed out that so-called tax "loopholes" were not illegal. They were simply the result of clever, highly knowledgeable lawyers carefully studying the tax code to find areas where the tax due could be greatly reduced or eliminated if an individual or company arranged to conduct their business or affairs in a certain way. One justice said that no one is obligated to arrange his affairs so as to pay the maximum tax. In fact, exactly the opposite is true; there is nothing illegal or immoral in arranging one's affairs so as to pay the minimum tax possible. He could have added, but didn't, that this is the reason tax lawyers, especially corporate tax lawyers, earn a lot of money—and are usually worth every penny.

Labor law is complicated, but not as complicated as the tax code. A good lawyer, or set of lawyers, can uncover a number of favorable things for either side as compared to their perceptions of what they can or cannot do. Efforts like this got underway in the 1970s as a result of management reactions to putting up with the new labor militants in the late 1960s and early 1970s. Reagan's actions with PATCO galvanized new efforts in this area. Rather than trying to avoid labor elections at all costs, companies began to see such elections as very good things if it meant getting rid of an undesirable union. Unions found a new hard-line attitude developing within management, and either their lawyers were not as good as those management engaged, or union officials were not as flexible in adopting new ways of doing things (the most likely result as their actions in the next two decades indicated). Unions began losing confrontations with management to a much greater degree.

The result of this effect (and the others noted above) was that unionized labor, as a percentage of the total work force, fell from 21.9 percent in 1980 to 16.1 percent in 1990. In addition, the total union work force fell in absolute terms, going from 19.8 million in 1980 to 16.7 million in 1990 (see

Appendix 1). This was the lowest percentage since the late 1930s, and the lowest total since the early 1950s, even though the total work force had almost doubled since the early 1950s. The Reagan years put the unions into free fall, and the fall would continue through the 1990s. Recovery is not in sight.

September 17, 1986—On this date the Senate confirmed Reagan's nomination of William Rehnquist as chief justice and Antonin Scalia as associate justice of the Supreme Court. In an era where disputes between organized labor and management were often settled in court, these confirmations put the conservatives more strongly in charge at the very top of the court system. But the hopes that unions could change their way of thinking about the management/labor interface in a way that would make using the court less often to reach a settlement were dashed in a series of negotiations around this time that bordered on the bizarre.

The first disappointment in the area came when GM announced plans to open a new plant in Spring Hill, Tennessee, later in the decade. The location was picked partly to keep it out of the (bad) influence of the Detroit atmosphere. GM planned to build their new Saturn car there, a car that would be built following the Japanese techniques of "quality circles" and "nonadversarial" relationships. Instead of bosses and workers there would be "advisers" and "associates." The intention would be to build cars that would match the Japanese legendary quality while being price-competitive.

The usual entire GM management contract was rewritten; including substituting for the hallowed management rights clause a phrase that said a "consensus decision-making process" would be used. While the details of getting the plant opened and running were being developed, a question was raised if it wasn't in fact illegal under the labor law as written in the United States for workers and managers not to have an adversarial relationship. The answer was no, but the fact the question was seriously asked showed how far apart the two sides had grown. Victor Reuther, brother of Walter Reuther, questioned in his memoirs the whole concept of the Saturn project. He felt that proposing a change in the usual adversarial relationship was nothing but a "scheme" to enable the company to sneak in speed-ups in production without the workers noticing. He said his brother Walter must be spinning in his grave at the thought of the UAW supporting a "corporate agenda based on competitiveness and all that."

Others pointed out that Walter Reuther had said that "experience has shown that there is no end to the variety and ingenuity of the methods management invents ... to quicken the work pace at the expense of the worker's health and safety." The union's job, first and foremost, was "eternal vigilance and militant resistance." This statement was from the 1950s, but it was treated as holy writ. One could easily imagine that unionism must be like a religion, not just an operating technique. Unionists constantly assumed that management was only concerned with more work done faster.

At least the Saturn agreement was signed in 1985; the plant was built, the cars are still in production there, and the two sides are continuing to learn how to make the new approach work. There still is hope a new approach can be developed.

July 15, 1987—On this date the United Food and Commercial Workers (UFCW) national union ended its trusteeship over the local union in Austin, Minnesota. This officially ended a "strike" that had been going on in the minds of the local P9 union since August 17, 1985, after Hormel had opened a new state-of-the-art plant that needed fewer than half the number of people used in the old plant. Wage cuts were also made due the change in the nature of the work. The national union agreed reluctantly to authorize the strike, but with the explicit exception of roving pickets and boycotts that were proposed which the national union knew were illegal. The local union, of course, proceeded to strike while ignoring the direction of the national union. The local union continued this policy through the strike.

On September 24 an administrative law judge ruled, on behalf of the National Labor Relations Board (NLRB), that local P9 was in violation of the law relative to the boycotts, and an injunction was issued the next day. On November 5 some relief was offered for the roving pickets if they could prove Hormel was not bargaining in good faith as the union claimed. On December 17 this offer was withdrawn, as no proof of bad faith was forthcoming. The national union also refused to supply funds for a Ray Rogers, a New York consultant who claimed to be able to tell unions how to conduct winning strikes. The national union considered him a charlatan and a fake that the local union had hired on its own.

In the middle of January 1986, after the local union turned down a "best and final" from Hormel, the company announced plans to reopen the plant with replacement workers if the union refused to return to work. This time the "no" vote was "2:1" per the union, while they claimed 93 percent voted "no" at the time of the strike last August. The UFCW told the local union they were "on the road to mass suicide" by refusing to go back to work. When the local workers got help to prevent the plant from opening, the UFCW put out a booklet attacking the local union leadership and its pied piper, Ray Rogers, and said that Hormel had been reasonable in its bargaining. By the end of January the governor of Minnesota provided enough troops to reopen the plant and it began to function again.

In a statement that would be laughable if it were not so sad, the P9 local union announced on January 29 they were going to implement tactics without the national union's (the UFCW) permission. They had yet to follow any of the directives of the UFCW from the beginning, which had put them in a strained position. They went back to the boycott route and roving pickets, and as the weeks went by the arrests and jail sentences followed as expected. The local union also managed to get 550 workers fired at other Hormel locations where P9 went to set up its illegal roving pickets. In the meantime, in response to a claim P9 misrepresented Hormel's contract offer to the local union, the governor provided a board to offer the contract in neutral terms. The local union refused to look at it.

But 10 days later, on February 11, the local P9 union made a counter-offer to Hormel. However, the company said no to agreeing to take everybody back, then announced it had a full operating complement in the plant with 650 replacement workers and 450 local union members who had crossed the picket line. The UFCW issued a statement condemning the strike and specifically calling Ray Rogers a "union-buster." Union P9 continued to strike—and break the law with their tactics. The UFCW had enough (P9 even sued their own top union for "malicious interference" with the strike), and a trusteeship hearing was held in Minnesota on April 14, and by May 8 the UFCW took over the local union through trusteeship. But the local union continued a frenzy of letter writing and lawsuits, and every move they made in terms of moving out of prior office buildings, turning over union assets, etc., generally required a specific court order. What it is they thought they were doing for their members is very hard to understand.

Maybe the answer was in a video interview with Ray Rogers held by reporters from the *New York Times* and the *Chicago Tribune* just after the local union P9 made its offer in February, 1986, to go back to work if Hormel took everyone back unconditionally (with a few other goodies thrown-in). The offer was a "ghost" in that Hormel had just fully restaffed the plant. Rogers appeared to think his offer was a wonderful thing. The reporters were incredulous and one asked Rogers the obvious question: "Do you mean to say that if this strike ends and no one gets his job back, you'll still declare it a victory?" Rogers responded, "However this turns out, there has been something very positive here...." The reporters shook their heads in disagreement and disbelief.

After the trusteeship ended on July 15,1987, as noted at the beginning of this entry, there were about 450 of the original local members (between 25 and 30 percent on the initial total) in the plant, and they were all members who had crossed the picket lines. The strikers had worked very hard for nothing, and the only way they knew how to conduct their strike was with illegal actions. Not a pretty story. But, unfortunately, a typical one for the 1980s and 1990s.

January 18, 1991—On this date Eastern Airlines declared bankruptcy. Eastern had been working on the edge of bankruptcy for nearly a decade, so this was not in itself a new story. What was new and is germane to this group of events illustrating notable strikes in the 1980s and 1990s that show the decline of organized labor is that bankruptcy was the goal of the machinists union at Eastern. They did not want their jobs back per se, they wanted to drive the company into bankruptcy to demonstrate that if things were not going to be done they way the union wanted, they were not going to be done at all. It was like the common story found in the newspapers all over the world every day. People fight to have things done their way.

The machinists were very angry with management. If they couldn't have the jobs at Eastern, no one could. Forget the thousands of people working at Eastern. The machinists were judge and jury. They destroyed the company to be sure no one but union people could have the jobs. In an economy with 84 percent of the people in the work force at the time not working in union jobs, a non-union company could not have been rare. But the machinists couldn't bear to see such a company, so they set out to destroy it. The fact that they killed their old jobs as well was irrelevant. Once again union members acted as if their union was more like a religion than an organized economical group.

A brief recent history of Eastern is needed to understand all the facts. As noted, Eastern had been on hard times in a very competitive industry for a long time. Frank Borman, the ex-Astronaut, had tried to turn the company around in the early 1980s, ending with a 1983 agreement with the three Eastern Unions, pilots, flight attendants, and machinists (by far the most disagreeable of the three), that would give the unions up to 25 percent of the stock in the company in exchange for some wage cuts and productivity goals. But the stock was finally put under the trusteeship of a judge who said he would vote it in the interests of the union rather than the stockholders. The company struggled onward, however.

In 1986, Texas Air Corporation bought out Eastern, as the stock trustee abstained on the vote to accept the offer from Texas Air. The unions wanted no part of Texas Air, owned by Frank Lorenzo, who was building up a large airline business by buying such companies as Continental Airlines, taking them into bankruptcy, then starting them up again as non-union airlines with very low operating costs. In the eyes of unions, Lorenzo was the ultimate ogre resulting from deregulation. Lorenzo took over Eastern and started the same wage cutting process after buying the company. The Eastern local of the International Association of Machinists (IAM) got the local unions of the pilots and stewardesses to go along with them, and they struck rather than accept pay cuts and the dismantling of union work rules. After all the gives and takes of negotiations as Lorenzo tried to absorb his new acquisition, it was March 4, 1989, before the union went out on strike. Lorenzo, having been through this before, placed the company under the protection of the bankruptcy court and started hiring replacement workers. The goal of the strike was then to prevent Eastern from ever emerging from bankruptcy. The IAM and the other unions decided they would throw their jobs in the pot to keep Lorenzo (or anybody else) from building a non-union airline. They didn't ask the workers already making a living at non-union airlines for their opinion. Like any religious organization there was no other way but the traditional way. The other non-union workers would have to make the same sacrifice whether they liked it or not.

At the top level, the national IAM and the AFL-CIO were not very enthusiastic about the local strike. After considering a national railroad strike to show sympathy and bring pressure on Eastern, the national officials backed off when courts began to talk about injunctions. It truly is amazing how, after all the years since the Taft-Hartley Act of 1947, the first move the unions think of is an illegal move. Then they thought of finding a "White Knight" to buy Eastern to whom they could offer even greater cuts than Lorenzo wanted to "keep the Eastern family together." It was clear that on a national level the idea of giving up all those jobs on the altar of avoiding a non-union company was not a good one if the jobs could be saved, even at a lower level of wages.

The Pilots showed signs of rationality when they ended their strike on November 22, 1989, "to save Eastern and get on with their lives." The IAM said they would "last one day longer than Lorenzo" to be sure Eastern would never make a profit with non-union labor. But on April 18, 1990, when the bankruptcy court removed Lorenzo from Eastern, the IAM decided to change its slogan to "one day longer" then Eastern. The airline had to die, it was written in the books of the IAM. They were claiming to act in the interest of workers everywhere, but they excluded the 84 percent who chose not to join a union. Another trustee was appointed by the bankruptcy court, but Eastern was finally forced to close and conduct a fire sale of its assets, which, of course, brought less money than an operating airline would have brought. Another group of suppliers and their workers who never got paid, no matter how small an operation they represented, were laid on the altar of the IAM in their quest to help the "little people" everywhere. The machinists, who took jobs where they could find them, had better hope no other fanatics like themselves show up to help them the way the IAM "helped" their "fellow workers."

Soon after the start of the strike, a newspaper ran a cartoon divided into a top and bottom block. In the top block it showed three figures in western garb each with a big six-shooter at their hip. The three figures had tee shirts identifying them as a machinist, a flight attendant, and a pilot. The machinist is saying "this time Lorenzo, we take no prisoners." The bottom block of the cartoon shows that each person has pulled his gun and placed it firmly against his head.

This strike is another example of why unions were disappearing through the 1990s. Absolutely no one gained anything from the strike, but the machinists considered themselves heroes and even wrote a book about their heroic acts (see Bibliography). A more rational look at the strike would conclude that with many more victories such as this, the war would soon be lost. And once again we have a local union deciding to go down in flames and take other workers with them as the national union looks on in dismay. Not a good trend for those trying to rebuild organized labor.

October 31, 1995—Sixteen years after being essentially appointed to the job by George Meany in 1979, Lane Kirkland was swept out of the Presidency of the AFL-CIO at its biennial October convention. Earlier in the year, dissidents had asked Kirkland to step down in favor of his next-in-charge Tom Donahue. Kirkland was being blamed for the free fall of organized labor, which started declining almost from the day he took charge. When Kirkland said no, the dissidents asked Donahue to run against Kirkland for the election, which was due in October. Donahue declined to take up a campaign against his boss, so John Sweeny, the head of the fast-growing Service International Employees Union (SIEU), one of the few growth unions in the Federation, offered to run.

Sweeny said that he decided to run because "organized labor is the voice of American workers and their families, and the silence I hear is deafening." His comment gave a name to the new organization the insurgents were putting together—"A New Voice for American Workers." The "New Voice" group added to the ticket Richard Trumka, current president of the United Mine Workers, who had a long history of militancy under the legendary John L. Lewis, and Linda Chavez-Thompson, vice-president of the American Federation of State, County, and Municipal Workers union. She represented women and people of color as each were under-represented in the hierarchy of the AFL-CIO.

Sweeny charged that the AFL-CIO was irrelevant to the "vast majority of unorganized workers," and he added that he felt it was rapidly becoming irrelevant to its own members as well. Kirkland finally saw that the new group was building support quickly and had an increasingly good chance to win, so he accepted their original demand and stepped down in favor of Donahue in August, 1995. But it was too late to stem the tide. The "New Voice" carried that day at the October convention, and, ironically it was the Reformers who had just taken over the long-time corrupt Teamsters Union that gave Sweeny his margin of victory.

On the anniversary of his election in 1996, Sweeny gave a speech telling business leaders that it was time for business and labor leaders to see each other "as natural allies, not natural enemies. American labor no longer takes the position that quality, productivity, and profits are not our business. They *are* our business. They are our jobs. And, indeed, they are our livelihoods." Even if the idea of cooperation with management was one that both Reuther brothers would have argued against it is an idea, or at least the expression of an idea, that gives hope to the concept that such an approach might work in the future.

This is a good place to give more examples of what Sweeny was up against. The PATCO strike debacle (see entry for August 5, 1981) is usually taken as the beginning of the fall, if not eventually the end, of organized labor in the United States. Labor was not prepared for the sudden action by Reagan, and its response was futile and failed miserably. But other analysts think the strike at Phelps Dodge just two years later in 1983 was more devastating in terms of showing how management had learned to defeat the unions in the new era.

In July 1983 the management of the Phelps Dodge copper mines in Arizona and Texas decided they could no longer afford the established system of an industry-wide wage and benefits pattern. The company refused to sign the pattern agreement established with other copper firms, and they demanded substantial concessions. A coalition of 13 unions, with the United Steelworkers in the lead, accordingly went on strike. The miners and the steelworkers had a long history of militancy, and a long battle was anticipated.

Nothing much happened in the first year as negotiations dragged on and each side postured in the "normal" way. But management had a plan in mind for the new era, and in July 1984 replacement workers were brought in. The miners organized mass picketing to defeat this move, but, as arranged, the governor of Arizona, George Babbitt, sent in state police to protect the replacement workers. When the "usual" violence broke out, the steelworker's top national leadership made it clear they wanted the strike to be conducted within the rules and violence or conflict with the authorities to be avoided.

With the strike a year old and the replacement workers doing the work, the company ordered a decertification election. In agreement with the law, strikers were not eligible to vote, and it was no surprise that the original union was decertified. While the new workers were running the mines under the new terms, the old workers were out on the street. The new company lawyers had played their cards correctly. The steelworkers union went to court, lost, and announced in September 1984 a new corporate campaign to withdraw funds from Phelp Dodge's major source of credit in two New York banks. A few months later, Albert Shanker pledged to do the same. But when the words "illegal boycott" began to wander through the air, Shanker went to the trouble of saying this withdrawal was not connected with Phelps Dodge, and then reneged on his pledge.

The steelworkers union held some rallies and talked about some related actions and then the whole business was silently dropped. The union at Phelps Dodge had been legally decertified and all the cries of "solidarity" were not going to change that fact. In essence, management had outsmarted the union, and without resorting to their old techniques of illegal action and defiance of authority, the union had no plan to offer a counter-attack. And the union that had lost so quickly and so cleanly was a respected union with a long history of fighting back and winning. It did not require a lot of insight for other unions to realize the same thing could happen to them. The President vs. PATCO had a lot of unique elements, but events like those at Phelps Dodge could happen anywhere the lawyers for the company did their homework and the union lawyers were taken by surprise. A new era had indeed dawned in the history of management-labor relationships, and slogans and illegal actions were not going to be enough for union victory in the new era. This is why so many labor analysts felt it was a more significant event than the PATCO strike.

Kirkland was blamed for Phelps Dodge and many other union losses that began to pile up in the 1980s and 1990s. There were a lot of things happening on the management side that were out of his control, but neither he nor his advisors could find good responses for management's new aggressive tactics. So Kirkland was out and Sweeny was in. Probably the events in just one city, Decatur, Illinois, in the 1990s, are enough to summarize the union/management battles going on before and after Sweeny's arrival on the scene. These events are in the entry that follows.

January 1, 1996—At the beginning of the first full year Sweeny was in charge of the AFL-CIO, three of his biggest problems were ongoing in Decatur, Illinois, where three strikes had become somewhat merged in the city of less than 100,000, if not in the plants themselves. We shall cover two of the three here.

The first was the one involved with Caterpillar, then the world's largest manufacturer of earth moving equipment. In 1989 Caterpillar had begun a restructuring program to stay competitive in the global market in which they competed. They cut their workforce by 30 percent, and built several new non-union plants. By 1991 only 25 percent of its total workforce consisted of United Automobile Workers (UAW), which had given Caterpillar high marks in its 1989 contract. But when Caterpillar asked for concessions, mainly including a two-tier pay scale for new hires in 1991, the UAW insisted that the company must meet the pattern already negotiated at John Deere, and when Caterpillar refused, the UAW struck in November 1991.

But the UAW ordered its workers back to work when, five months into the strike, Caterpillar threatened to bring in replacement workers. Caterpillar jobs were attractive because of their high pay, especially in Decatur where two other major strikes were going on. The UAW worked for two-and-a-half years without a contract under Caterpillar terms, but the UAW began to flood the National Labor Relations Board (NRLB) with unfair-labor-practice complaints. Finally, in June 1994, the UAW ordered its members back out on strike. Caterpillar began to hire replacement workers.

The company took the usual steps in such a case by ordering managers to work temporarily on the production lines, and, in addition to adding new hires, contract workers, and union members who crossed the picket lines, they opened the production jobs for internal bidding to their office and clerical workers. The big, burly men who ran the big assembly machines and the actual big machines themselves as they neared final assembly, smirked and sneered when their jobs were opened to the (mostly) women clerical and office workers. But these workers could not run fast enough to the application lines when they saw the huge salaries that were available compared to what they made up front in the office. These women typically ran several different software programs on the word processors they used in their work, and they were used to answering the anguished screams of their bosses who wanted to transfer someone or set up a conference call on their high technology telephone systems, or needed to send a fax or an e-mail.

When the women found out these big strong men in production, with their big fat paychecks, spent most of their time pushing buttons to control the computers that operated the machinery, they though they had found the door to heaven. In no time they were pushing the right buttons at the right time, and on payday they had some real money to take home to the children many of them were raising alone. The big, burly men found that their smirks vanished amazingly fast.

The industry spread the word about Caterpillar. John Deere, the competitor whom Caterpillar was supposed to follow as a pattern, decided it would be better to follow the example of Caterpillar, and started pressing for concessions from the union. As almost always happens in cases of this kind, when Caterpillar starting filling first what they felt were the most critical positions to get up and running again, they found that when they reached an acceptable production level, they still had open personnel requisitions. They weren't exactly sure what these other people used to do, but they canceled those requisitions right away. Nearly always when you restaff from scratch, you find you need substantially fewer people.

In desperation, after 17 months on strike in December 1995, the UAW negotiated a new agreement with Caterpillar. Caterpillar's workers turned it down by 80 percent. Those ex-clerical workers were fond of those big new paychecks. The UAW then "recessed" the strike and ordered the workers back to work on essentially whatever terms Caterpillar offered. They specifically gave Caterpillar the unilateral right to reject grievances they found to be "frivolous or repetitive." It obviously was an item that was needed, because the only thing the UAW had to show for its strike even a year later was a backlog of cases, true or not, that the NRLB had to rule on that claimed unfair labor practices. Lawyers vs. lawyers, once again. The company, in the meantime, was operating profitably.

At nearly the same time in Decatur that the UAW struck Caterpillar in 1994, the Staley Company, which had been taken over by a British Company in 1988, was in the midst of a battle with their union. Instead of striking against a contract the union did not like in September 1992, the union went on a work-to-rule campaign, an ancient union tactic (the IWW proposed a similar idea 80 years ago, but they added sabotage to the mix) where no one works efficiently, claiming to work just as the rules, as they interpret them, tell them to. The workers claimed they managed to cut production by one-third to one-half, so, not surprisingly, Staley locked out all 760 workers in June 1993. The strike turned ugly in June 1994 when police used pepper spray to prevent the strikers from blocking the gates of the plant where replacement workers were working. Once again the union had called in the agitator-consultants, Ray Rogers and Jerry Tucker, and once again the top national union leaders had the local union throw them out in January 1995.

The company made an offer similar to the first one, and it failed by only 57 percent as opposed to the 97 percent three years before. On December 12, 1995, Jim Shinall, a former union officer who had previously called for a settlement so he and older workers could retire, was voted president of the local union. This time essentially the same contract was approved by 56 percent (Shinall retired in April as he had previously announced). The vote was directed by the national union, and that was the end of the strike. Only one-quarter of the Staley workers took back their jobs, and the rest either retired or went to other jobs.

Once again, using the old, old strategies of the past along with the new pied pipers of union consultants at the express opposition of the national union, the local strikers gained absolutely nothing. This was the kind of thing Sweeny was facing. Not so much a decline of organized labor, but a desperate urge to commit suicide in battle just as some religious fanatics insist on doing. Sweeny had a task in front of him that perhaps no man could handle.

September 11, 2001—This was the new day of infamy for the United States when terrorists destroyed the World Trade Towers in New York. Although it has since been shown that the recession following the bombing had actually started a few months before the event, airlines and all parts of the travel and entertainment business were especially hard hit. Needless to say the recession made it hard for unions not to be faced with wage cutbacks and similar problems. But unions with operating techniques from the dark ages like the International Association of Machinists (IAM), who gave us the Eastern Airlines bankruptcy in which they destroyed their own jobs, now threatened strikes against United Airlines, whose survival was clearly in doubt (and which is actually owned by its unions, including the IAM).

Admittedly, the machinists were long overdue for a raise, but the nasty act on September 11 brought a lot of hard times to a lot of people through no fault of their own. As 2002 began, and the machinists persisted, organized labor recognized the possibility that they might be treated to the spectacle of a union preparing to essentially to strike itself. This issue will be discussed further in the items covering 2002 and after, but it was yet another issue of another type for Sweeny to deal with. It would be hard to blame him for proposing that the IAM should be put in a separate labor category of its own. It seemed that this particular union was concerned only with its best interest and not that of organized labor.

October 3, 2001—The *Los Angeles Times* carried an article announcing that the United Automobile Workers Union (UAW) lost its bid to represent the workers at the Nissan automobile plant in Smyrna, Tennessee. It was the fourth time in 12 years that the UAW lost in an attempt to organize the factory, which would have marked the first time the UAW organized a factory in the United States that was fully owned by a foreign company. It was only the second time in those four attempts that the UAW even got as far as being authorized to hold an election, and they lost this time by a margin of more than 2 to 1, with 67.6 percent of the 4,589 workers (3,103) voting no. The result was about the same as it was in 1989, when 69.5 percent of the workers voted no. The plant originally opened in 1983.

Labor experts said the loss put the UAW back at "square one" in trying to organize any of the factories built in the United States by Japan and Germany (or anyone else) to produce cars here. The experts said the size of the loss in the election makes it unlikely the UAW will succeed anytime in the near future in organizing any of the foreign built plants.

The UAW put a brave face on the loss saying they still have great strength among the typical "Big Three" automakers, GM, Ford, and Chrysler (now owned by Germany's DaimlerChrysler). But the total membership of the UAW fell to 700,000 last year. Their membership was about 1.5 million 20 years ago, not far from their all-time peak of near 1.6 million.

December 4, 2001—The top United States Steel Company, the U.S. Steel Group of USX, said it was discussing a consolidation of five major producers in the United States into one steel company that would be three times the size of U.S. Steel. This would give the new company sufficient size to compete in the international market. But help from the federal government would be needed both to fend off anti-trust charges and to carry the burden of the retiree pension and health cost of the companies.

These retiree costs, known as legacy costs, are one of the biggest problems the once-dominant steel industry faces in the United States. At its peak in the late 1970s, the industry employed about 580,000 workers. Today it employs about 142,000. It is estimated that the top five companies alone face unfunded pension and health costs of $10 billion dollars. But analysts warned that any proposal for federal help would have to include agreements to rid the industry of inefficient plants and excess capacity.

Any merger deal, according to U.S. Steel, would require "progressive new labor agreements that would provide for meaningful reductions in costs." Leo W. Gerald, president of the United Steelworkers of America, said the union was ready to talk about any restructuring plan as long as it preserves jobs. The union said 27,000 jobs have been lost since January 1998, nearly 11,000 of which were lost in the first seven months of 2001.

A government representative said to avoid anti-trust problems, the merger would have to show they would not dominate their market, which would mean the new company would have to claim its market is the world, in which the United States looks "like little potatoes." But if the merger gains the trade restrictions it is asking, it would be hard to argue it is competing against the world.

The true unpleasant facts are that the United States has a steel making capacity of about 126 million tons a year, while worldwide capacity is 900 million tons a year, a small share of the total. Further, the United States steel industry can supply only about three-quarters of the total amount of steel needed just by the manufacturers in the United States. They can't compete (often on price) internationally, and they're not even big enough to supply their home market if no one else was allowed in. No matter how pretty a picture one tries to paint, this usually describes a dying industry. But the president of the industry union sounds more than ready to do whatever it takes to assure that no jobs are lost. Somewhere along the way the unions have lost touch with reality. There may be a solution somewhere requiring plants to merge, which always means getting rid of excess layers of management, and requiring layoffs as well among union workers. But that solution will not be found if all parties are not looking for it. Jobs only exist when there is work to be done. At least among efficient companies.

December 5, 2001—The *Los Angeles Times* carried an article describing the problems at United Airlines. Their new CEO, John Creighton, had a honeymoon of about one month before grumbling from the unions (which own 55 percent of United) reached critical levels. The pilots got a fat wage increase last summer, but they are unwilling to cut any of that until they see management make other cuts at the top. The mechanics are after a gain as well, and they threaten to strike if they don't get it. Like the pilots, they refuse to talk about future concessions until they have the new wage in their pocket.

A similar scenario happened in the early 1990s when the unions took deep wage concessions in exchange for 55 percent of the stock in the company. But United has the second-highest operating costs per seat mile in the industry, and the loss of revenue caused by the events of September 11, 2001, is giving the airline an especially bright red shade of losses.

The company has enough assets to avoid immediate bankruptcy, but the biggest unions are insisting on good wage increases before considering any wage concessions. Maybe the union should increase its share of the carrier to 100 percent in exchange for more concessions, then everyone would get to see if union owners could come up with creative new ideas in dealing with the operating unions. Everyone might learn something.

December 6, 2001—The AFL-CIO held its biannual convention this week in Las Vegas, the third since John Sweeny was elected president of the federation in 1995 with high hopes he could turn around the ongoing decline of organized labor. Alas, for labor, the mood was somber. The American economy had been strong during most of that time and millions of new jobs were created, but most were non-union jobs. Gains of 2.5 million union jobs were made since 1955, but the losses were larger.

As shown in the Appendix, in 1995, unions represented 14.9 percent of the total work force. By 2000, it was down to 13.5 percent (the total number of union members fell from 16.360 million to 16.258 million). In 2001 the percentage held steady at 13.5 percent, and the total grew to 16.28 million workers, almost exactly the same as in 2000. Actually, in a sense, it was even worse. Back in 1955 public sector unions were mostly unknown. Today public sector unions have grown substantially, and "the standard blue collar" union members are now below 10 percent of the total work force. It's the public sector that keeps the overall percentage in the low teens, with police officers, firefighters, and other protective service workers having a unionized rate of 38 percent. In 1983, the first year truly comparable figures are available, union rates had fallen from 20.1 percent to 13.6 percent. This is quite similar to the lumped numbers shown in Appendix I for that period. But it does mean that the peak of 35.5 percent reached in 1945 is now below 10 percent. Any organization that falls from nearly 40 percent to below 10 percent of the group in which it competes is struggling for survival.

The facts are the facts. Unions are in severe decline. A book published in 2001 titled *Rekindling the Movement* with a sub-title of "Labor's quest for relevance in the 21st century" (see Bibliography) is a summary of articles and

December 6, 2001

essays by labor analysts and professors addressing the issues raised by the title and sub-title of the book. It is taken as a given that unions are, and have been, in severe decline. The key question is whether their decline can be stopped at the point where they are still at least a relevant force in today's economy. The book is, as are most books written about unions, decidedly pro-union. But this book is more objective than most, and it puts its pro-union bias in the context of an academic belief that the country is better off with a strong union movement than without one. It is otherwise straightforward.

There are plenty of union strike success stories, such as the UPS strike of 1997, where the Teamsters union prepared carefully, put its alliances in order in advance, and carried out its strike actions in a mostly legal way. It also had a popular issue in trying to reverse the habit corporations had of hiring "temporary employees" at reduced wages and benefits, and then leaving them defined as "temporary" for as long as a decade or more. It was a very successful strike for labor, in contrast to some of the horror stories we have reviewed in this part of the book. It was labor's biggest win in more than a decade at the time.

But most of the success stories (and failures) are on a much smaller scale (the *Rekindling* book also briefly mentions many of the horror stories we have discussed in this book, referring to them almost in the sense of ugly legends from the past that must be avoided at all costs in the future because labor has declined partly due to ugly strikes such as these). The bottom line was that in the UPS strike the unions carefully planned how they would work together, and they avoided clearly illegal actions like the plague. Their success story sounded much like those won by management in terms of how management won. Careful planning and study of what the rules were, and the avoidance of illegal actions. It is not necessary to clog the streets and traffic, to file hundreds of (true or not) papers claiming "unfair labor practices," and generally to behave as if the key strategy was to be such a nuisance that for years the company would pay you to go away (settle). That is how it was done in the very old days, but these are the new days.

The conclusion one reaches from this and many other books (see the Bibliography) is that there are two key things unions need to learn to do to make a comeback. The first is to try to cooperate with management and get rid of the sense that there simply has to be an adversarial relationship. This was the sense of the speech Sweeny gave on his second anniversary (see entry for October 31, 1995). Unions have often viewed management as an adversary to be reckoned with. A force that only exists to push workers to produce more and work at a faster rate.

Sweeny's speech was right on the mark. Profits are everyone's concern, not just managements. Over 90 percent of the companies in the United States have found it easier to generate profits without being encumbered with a union. There's a message there. And many of these companies are making millionaires of their employees with everyone focusing on the southeast corner of the profit-and-loss statement. So it's not just a question of cutting wages—it's quite the reverse. If the unions cannot learn this lesson, they truly will become irrelevant to the nation's economy, and it's not impossible they have already arrived at that point.

The second key point is that the unions need to learn to offer some reason for people to join them. In a sense, the unions have been too successful. Many of the things they once fought for (the eight hour day, overtime rules, unemployment compensation, health care, pensions, safety on the job, a minimum wage, etc.) are now provided by federal and state (often both) statutes. Huge bureaucracies like OSHA (safety) and ERISA (pensions) operate nationally. The "safety net" or the "welfare state," depending on your point of view, is the reason the number of women employed in the work force is now essentially 50 percent (see Appendix 3). This is because the majority of the workers employed in these areas are women, and the need for more workers grow each time Congress passes another pile of "welfare state" bills.

The union is not the place people go when they are laid-off or in need of financial aid. Instead, the people go to some state or federal agency. To them the unions are, in fact, irrelevant. The unions completely reversed the view of illegal aliens in their attempt to sign new members. The unions used to be strongly opposed to illegal aliens because they saw them as competition for jobs and who were willing to accept low wages. As soon as unions saw illegal aliens as potential new members instead, the unions clamored for amnesty and more liberal immigration laws. Just as in the last centuries, the unions suddenly realized these "illegals" could use assistance finding their way into the welfare state. If unions want to persist in this direction, offering classes in English and some basic job skills to people who have almost no useful skills at all would be a reason for joining a union. The CIO got off to a fast start in the 1930s by signing up members without requiring the payment of dues on the basis members should not pay until the union did something for them. It was a new approach. It may not be applicable now, but it was new then.

Some sort of new thinking that would show management why they would be better off with unions than without would prove helpful to the unions. Whether there are any answers or not is hard to say. Certainly, putting some energy into thinking about how unions could be a positive rather than a negative would help the interface between management and unions. If unions are unable to think of new ways of doing things along these lines, unions are already in their death spiral. It will take a long time for unions to fade away completely in the private sector, but without new thinking a day will come when people who remember when there were unions in the private sector will find it hard to recall what useful purpose they served.

December 27, 2001—*Los Angeles Times* sports columnist J. A. Adande, commenting on the way the Baseball Players Union examination of the deferred money involved in the trade of Mo Vaughn of the California Angels to the New York Mets (an arrangement satisfactory to all three parties) dragged out the consummation of the trade even though it was questionable if the union had any jurisdiction in the area they were questioning, said that the whole business reminded him of the famous book by scientist Richard Dawkins called *The Selfish Gene*. The book argues that the driving force in life is the DNA molecule, and that "everything else—from humans to goldfish—exists merely to help the genes survive."

In Andane's mind, this "pretty much matches the view of the union, which thinks that major league baseball, the stadiums, (and) the television contracts all exist solely to further (the union's) own ends." This statement from a sports columnist, who are known for their dislike of owners and who usually side with the players in any dispute because of their closeness to some of the players and the fact that most reporters are also in a union, is worthy of note. It is a warning to the players' union that their arrogance is getting out of hand in a way that even their usual supporters notice.

The baseball players' union has more confidence than most unions because the owners have never used replacement players in a dispute. The union claims the players are irreplaceable. But they ignore that 50 years ago players like Joe DiMaggio was winding up his career, players like Ted Williams and Stan Musial were in their prime, and young players like Willie Mays and Hank Aaron were just getting started. These players are all in the Hall of Fame, they have moved on to retirement, and they have been adequately replaced by new Hall of Famers. None of us are irreplaceable. The union claims credit for the great increase in salaries over the years, but it is the free agent system and aggressive agents that have accomplished this, not the union (although they did play a role in launching the free agent system). One year of replacement players would make the baseball players' union much more cooperative. All other major league sports operations have lived quite well with a salary cap, for example, but the baseball players' union refuses to agree to such.

January 1, 2002—The minimum wage in California rose to $6.75 an hour, matching Massachusetts for the second highest in the nation behind the state of Washington, and an even $1.60 above the federally mandated rate. There have been ongoing arguments for years about whether a higher minimum wage helps workers at the bottom of the pay scale, or actually hurts them by making small business owners shy away from hiring such workers because they become too expensive, by forcing up wages in general as other workers expect a "bounce" as well (a minimum wage of $6.75 per hour is $270 per week, or over $14,000 per year). The argument goes on and on.

But the point of including this item here is to note again how state and federal statutes have taken over what was once a prime goal of unions. No one had to do anything; the minimum wage just went up automatically. Another item to add to the list of why unions are no longer relevant in today's liberal world. Many of their functions have been taken over by the welfare state. It's hard to imagine any state or federal body reducing the minimum wage in today's economy, let alone trying to eliminate it. The rate at which the minimum wage increases with time can be dependent on the nature of a given legislative body in terms of how liberal or conservative it may be. But the minimum wage, and its increases over time, is here to stay. No lack of union action will cause it to shrink or go away.

January 23, 2002—An article in the *Los Angeles Times* noted that China leads the world in coal production—and in the number of lives lost trying to extract coal from the earth. The United States is believed to actually have more coal in the ground than anyone, but with coal being replaced with oil and gas as an energy source in the United States, China produces more coal than any other nation, with the United States a close second.

Again in the category of what unions used to do before federal and state statutes took over, coal mining in the United States used to be a very dangerous business. But following the lead of the coal mining unions, there are now numerous safety laws in place. For example, in China at least 5,400 hundred known deaths took place in the mines in the first 11 months of the year, and this is not a number China likes to give great visibility to. Estimates are that 10,000 deaths per year occur in the coal mining process in China. In the United States, with an almost equal rate of production, there are about 30 mining deaths each year.

That means the death rate in China is 333 times as high as in the States. What the miners in China badly need today is their own public figure to fight for their rights. The low death rate number in the States owes much to the work of John L. Lewis and his followers in the first half of century. The good news is that in terms of safety the job done by Lewis has passed on to OSHA and similar government groups. And the miners that are not killed but injured have a much better care and support system mandated by the government than even John L. Lewis could have dreamed of. One death is one too many, but having Lewis with us today would not be likely to change the present death rate much. And neither would have the union disappear. The hands of the state and federal governments have, once again, replaced those of the union.

January 24, 2002—A new California state agency that would pull together the Economic Development Department, the Department of Industrial

Relations, the Agricultural Labor Relations Board, and the Workforce Investment Board, was announced to be up and running by mid-summer of this year. This new agency would pull together "34 different programs in 13 different agencies." To help get the votes needed to create the new "umbrella" group, the Fair Employment and Housing Departments, which handle discrimination complaints, would be left standing as they are.

In the future, attempts will be made to consolidate state and federally funded job training and vocation education programs, which are now run by a "hodgepodge" of groups. This was not considered an announcement of great moment, just a program taking a nick here and a tuck there for greater efficiency of operation.

February 1, 2002—It was announced that a five-year campaign to unionize the flight attendants at Delta Airlines failed after a vote count on this day. The union responded that the vote was "unfair" (union protocol calls for any vote they lose to be denounced as "unfair"—the last time any union has owned up to losing a "fair" vote is not known). At any rate, the National Mediation Board started the process to consider a new vote, a process one assumes that will continue until the union gets a result they like. For the moment the anti-union consultants hired by Delta for $2.5 million hold an edge over the 50,000 flight attendants in the Association of Flight Attendants who put the campaign together to back the union.

Delta has a total of 19,033 flight attendants, so the vote of only 5,520 that was placed in the "yes" column meant that the resulting "no" vote was 71 percent, an overwhelming margin. But this is the normal practice today. If at least one person votes yes for the union, the standard action by the union is to suggest that all the rest meant to do so but were swayed from doing so in some "unfair" way.

February 2, 2002—United Airlines announced its biggest loss ever, even though the fourth quarter came in a little better than expected. The total loss for the year was $2.1 billion, the biggest ever for any airline in history. The major airlines in the United States lost a total of more than $7 billion in 2001, with United the last to report. As a leading carrier for businessmen, United has been especially hurt by the recession that was deepened by the events of September 11, 2001. United executives said that the carrier is losing about $10.6 million a day. It has about $2.6 billion in cash to tide it over to put its rescue plan into effect.

Unfortunately its plan requires achieving large cuts in wages from United's employees, who account for 40 percent of United's costs. The employees also own 55 percent of United's stock, so one would assume something could be worked out. However, the machinists' union, which represent

15,000 United employees, first want a huge wage increase (such as the pilots got the summer before the World Trade Towers were destroyed) before they will agree to even talk about concessions. Unless the concessions are bigger than the increase, no net savings will result. At any rate, a presidential board has backed pay hikes for the machinists (the machinists have been without a raise since the early 1990s when they took stock in lieu of cash). But the union has said they may not approve the increase recommended by the board, because, like all unions since the time of Samuel Gompers over a century ago, they want "more and more." The prior record for a one-year loss had been set at $1.23 billion by Continental Airlines in 1990, but this year US Airways lost $1.97 billion and American Airlines lost $1.8 billion before United made its report. In such an atmosphere the new cooperation between management and labor that new AFL-CIO president John Sweeny talked about on his one year anniversary in 1996 (see entry for October 31, 1955) would be a good way to save the airlines and continue to have airline jobs available in the United States. So far the new cooperation looks a lot like the old battles between labor and management.

February 7, 2002—The census department announced that the percent of the total population that was foreign born in the 2000 census jumped to 10 percent, the highest census level since 1930. This is still below the record levels of 15 percent in 1890 and 1910, and below all the years since it reached 10 percent in 1850 and stayed in the low teens through the 1930s, dropping to 9 percent in 1940.

This explains why, as noted before, the AFL-CIO has switched from opposing illegal immigrants, once seen as low-cost job competitors, to embracing immigration of all kinds now that immigrants are seen as potential union members. But today's immigrants tend to settle in the south and west rather than the northeast and midwest as they did in the later 1880s. They also take jobs in the lower wage fields of harvesting crops, doing lawn work, cleaning and serving in expensive hotels and resorts, and providing janitorial services in high rise office building offices. These are jobs requiring few, if any, skills, and the immigrants are easily replaced by just about anyone who will work for less. Such groups are not easily organized into viable unions.

The unions are continually looking for new members. Except for liberal cities like Santa Monica, California, known locally as "the People's Republic of Santa Monica," it is hard to get much local support for organizing the immigrants, legal or illegal. After all, one attractive feature of some immigrants for local businesses is that they work cheaper. Unionized immigrants soon lose that advantage because they have to pay to support the local union bureaucracy. Trying to rebuild union strength on a base of immigrants doesn't hold a lot of promise for a turnaround in union relevance.

February 14, 2002—The mechanics at United Airlines refused to accept a contract proposed by a presidential emergency board. The mechanics believe they can get "more" than the 37 percent raise offered this year in the proposed contract. Analysts said they believe the mechanics "seem to be on a suicide mission that could take the company down if the rejection leads to a strike." At a minimum United would be expected to file for bankruptcy to protect its assets. Since the United unions own 55 percent of the company, they would be in essence striking against themselves. But the mechanics drove Eastern into bankruptcy 20 years ago even though they owned part of that company, as well, so the mechanics are more than capable of driving the airline to bankruptcy.

March 5, 2002—President Bush announced plans to impose tariffs of up to 30 percent on imported steel to help the present emergency in the steel business (see entry for December 4, 2001). The intent is to give the steel companies breathing space to retool and close inefficient plants to be able to compete in world markets. In the meantime it will increase the cost of steel by as much as 10 percent in the United States, and possibly endanger jobs in industries heavily dependent on the cost of steel.

This may be a first step for the 2004 presidential election rather than a realistic plan to rescue the steel industry in the United States, where 31 companies have initiated bankruptcy proceedings in the last four years, but it should at least extend the life span a little for the dying industry, depending on what response other countries decide to make.

March 6, 2002—Many news operations carried today the announcement that United Airlines and its mechanics union released yesterday that they had ratified an agreement that will permit the carrier to keep flying. If the mechanics union keeps its word, the airline can move on the next step of trying to get the pilots and the mechanics to give back enough of the big increases they received this year to give the airline a chance to break even. At least United is still flying, and that's a big accomplishment, all things considered.

Whatever the outcome of the United battle, this chronology shows the question that the AFL-CIO is asking itself as to whether unions are still relevant in today's world and can recapture their prior growth can be answered with a resounding no! Is there any sign unions in general are trying to follow the spirit of the first anniversary speech by President John Sweeny of the AFL-CIO (see entry for October 31, 1955)?

Other than the "religious" feelings that a country should have private sector unions because they've had them for a long time, and they are a "traditional" part of the landscape, there are no objective reasons for their existence. They once were needed, and did a good job overall in improving the lot of the "blue collar" worker. But today they are an anachronism whose time has passed. As in the United Airlines situation, where they actually own the company, they are the company's single biggest problem. It may be that before long the actions of the unions will lead to their own demise.

Public sector unions may last for a longer time because the rules they work under generally make it easier to deal with them. Simply enforcing the "no strike" rules may be enough to enable them to function as a convenient central point to negotiate with the workforce as a whole. But it seems that private sector unions have had their day.

Appendix 1: Percentage of Union Membership in Work Force 1930–2000

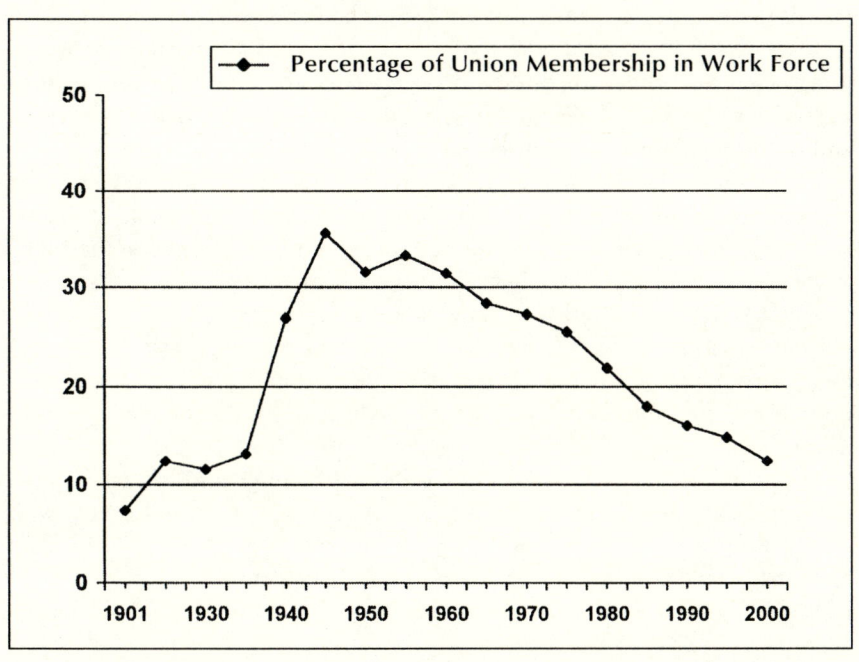

1. Union Membership

U.S. UNION MEMBERSHIP IN WORK FORCE 1930–2000

Year	Labor Force (thousands)	Union Members (thousands)	Percentage of Labor Force	Year	Labor Force (thousands)	Union Members (thousands)	Percentage of Labor Force
1901	19,000	1,000	7.3	1965	60,815	17,299	28.4
1920	40,000	5,000	12.5	1970	70,920	19,381	27.3
1930	29,424	3,401	11.6	1975	76,945	19,611	25.5
1935	27,053	3,584	13.2	1980	90,564	19,843	21.9
1940	32,376	8,717	26.9	1985	94,524	16,996	18.0
1945	40,394	14,322	35.5	1990	103,905	16,740	16.1
1950	45,222	14,267	31.5	1995	110,038	16,360	14.9
1955	50,675	16,802	33.2	2000	120,786	16,258	13.5
1960	54,234	17,049	31.4				

SOURCE: BUREAU OF LABOR STATISTICS

The percentage of union membership in the workforce shows that in 1901 unions had only reached 7.3 percent of the total workforce (excluding farm workers and the unemployed). The unions grew during World War I (which is typical of the wartime workforce), but then stayed relatively flat through the 1920s and early 1930s as the depression began. The implementation of the Wagner Act in 1935–1937 caused a big boom in unions, and with World War II following immediately, unions grew to 35.5 percent of the workforce as the war ended in 1945. The excesses of the unions in the form of strikes from 1945–1946 resulted in the anti-labor Taft-Hartley Act in 1947, and union membership began to fall slowly from that date forward.

The merger of the AFL and CIO in 1955 held the unions together for a few more decades but with a diminishing percent of the total. Response by management to the militants that appeared in the workforce in the 1960s and 1970s started a sharper decline in union membership, and President Reagan's firing of the Air Traffic Controllers in 1981 triggered an even sharper decline as management followed his cue of being more aggressive in applying the labor laws in ways that were favorable to them. Labor seemed to have no new response to this except more of the usual—strikes and disruption of normal work.

The AFL-CIO threw out its old leadership in 1995, and at least stopped the decline in total membership, but the percentage of the workforce who were union members continued to fall. This stands at 13.5 percent today, but unions in the public sector are holding the percentage up. In the "conventional" private sector, the percentage has fallen below 10 percent, probably eventually on its way to zero.

The "revolution" of the 1930s under the Roosevelt Administration also added laws regulating employment for women, child labor laws, unemployment compensation, minimum wages, average hours worked, safety rules, and similar factors affecting labor. Laws regarding several of these items had been passed previously but were found unconstitutional by the Supreme Court. In the later 1930s they finally passed constitutional muster. And then, as the Wagner Act became fully implemented, several of these items became part of the negotiations between the unions and the companies.

There were mixed feelings about the child labor laws because in the depression every penny of income was needed by many families, but organized labor had always supported this issue, just as organized labor always supported compulsory, free education. It kept children off the labor market, but more importantly most workers knew it was the only way their children would get an education and a chance for a better life.

Social Security was also implemented in the revolution of the 1930s as the first real pension plan the common worker ever held, although pension plans beyond the wildest expectations of most workers would grow out of the negotiations with GM and Ford pushed by Walter Reuther after World War II. In summation, just about every aspect of life affecting organized labor other than "conventional" issues like wages and working conditions got their start (on a permanent basis) in the revolution of the 1930s.

APPENDIX 2: DECLINE IN U.S. FARM WORKERS 1820–1994

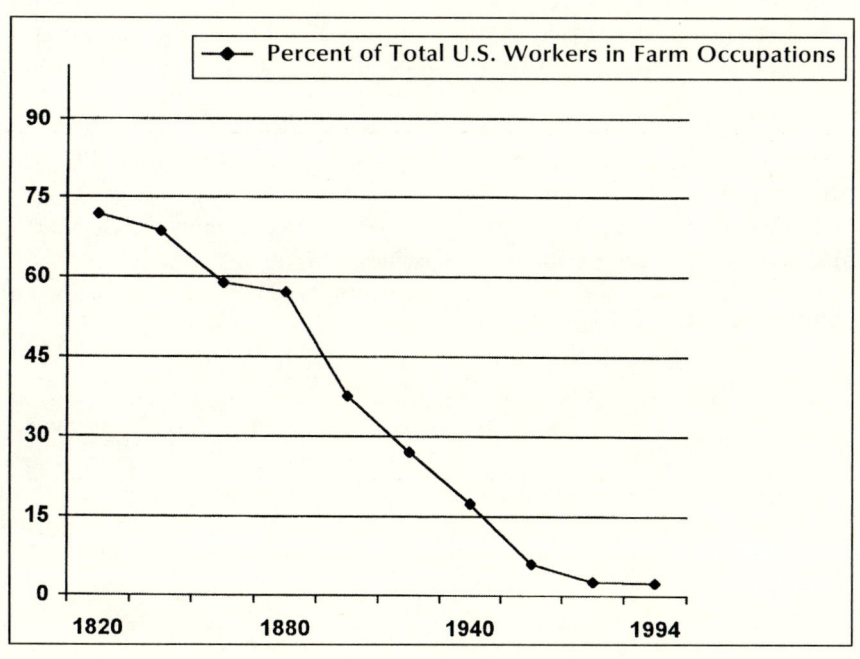

2. Decline in Farm Workers

PERCENT OF TOTAL U.S. WORKERS IN FARM OCCUPATIONS 1820–1994

Year	Percent of U.S. Workers in Farm Occupations	Year	Percent of U.S. Workers in Farm Occupations
1820	71.8	1920	27.0
1840	68.6	1940	17.4
1860	58.9	1960	6.1
1880	57.1	1980	2.7
1900	37.5	1994	2.5

SOURCE: U.S. Department of Agriculture

The decline in farm workers shows clearly how quickly the United States became a manufacturing nation following the Industrial Revolution that was given a big boost by the inventions of Eli Whitney around 1800 as described in the Introduction. Even as late as 1820 almost three-quarters of the workforce was involved in farming, but as the railroads began to roll across the nation after the Civil War, the percentage was down to about 58 percent, and by the turn of the century the percentage was almost exactly half of what it had been in 1820. When World War II started only 17 percent of the work force was needed to produce the nation's food, and in just 20 more years it was down to six percent. Today only 2.5 percent of the nation's workforce is producing the nation's food, with much left over to ship overseas.

The sharpest drops came between 1940 and 1960, when farm work fell from 17.4 to 6.1 percent, a drop of 65 percent, and in the next 20 years between 1960 and 1980 when it fell from 6.1 percent to 2.7 percent, a drop of 56 percent. Overall, between 1940 and 1980, the percentage of the workforce involved in farm production fell by nearly 85 percent. After the nation tooled up for World War II, people stayed employed in the manufacturing and service areas, and farm occupations essentially vanished.

Appendix 3: Percentage of Women in the U.S. Work Force 1870–2000

PERCENTAGE OF WOMEN IN THE U.S. WORK FORCE 1870–2000

Year	Percentage	Year	Percentage
1870	15.3	1940	25.4
1880	16.2	1950	29.6
1890	17.7	1960	34.6
1900	18.3	1970	39.2
1910	21.6	1980	43.2
1920	21.5	1990	46.1
1930	22.4	2000	46.4

SOURCE: Bureau of Labor Statistics

The percentage of women employed in the workforce grew at a surprising flat rate from the late 1800s. The heroes of the early women's movement were women like Elizabeth Carrie Stanton, Susan B. Anthony, Elizabeth Gurley Flynn, Jane Addams, Alice Paul, and Carrie Chapman Catt who made various contributions towards getting women the vote. After that was officially achieved on August 18, 1920, women were able to encourage the passage of numerous laws that enabled them to be treated as persons instead of property. Nothing energizes a politician like a voter, especially one who seems to be potentially part of a block vote.

Getting the vote also increased the level of women in the labor force. By 1920, the percentage of women in the workforce had risen from 15.3 percent in 1870 to 21.5 percent in 1920, an increase of 6.2 percentage points on an absolute basis in 50 years (an increase of just over 40 percent on a rate basis). In the next 50 years, the percentage went from 21.5 in 1920 to 39.2 in 1970, an increase on an absolute basis of 17.7 percentage points, and an increase on a rate basis of over 82 percent.

In the first 40 years from 1920 to 1960 after women received voting power they added 13.1 percentage points on an absolute basis and 61 percent on a rate basis. In the following 40 years to 2000, they added 11.8 percentage points on an absolute basis, and only 34 percent on a rate basis. But the rate of increase has to be expected to slow down as women approach equity in the total count, i.e.; women are closer to occupying 50 percent of the work force. Issues of "equal pay" and "glass ceilings" aside, women and men are already nearly equal when it comes to representation in the work force.

However, 80 percent of "clerical" occupations are held by women, as are 60 percent of "service" occupations, and these are relatively low paying jobs. Only 17 percent of women hold jobs in what would generally be considered "blue collar" occupations, where the pay is generally higher. Overall, the biggest occupation by far is managerial, technical, and sales—all "white collar" occupations, at 60 percent of the total workforce. What have traditionally been "blue collar" jobs represent 25 percent in total, and "service" jobs represent the remaining 15 percent. But the "bluest" of the "blue collar" jobs rank even with the service jobs at roughly 15 percent, and the "service" category could include many more jobs from the managerial, technical, and sales category depending on how one wished to define them.

Appendix 4:
Work Stoppages Involving 1,000 Workers or More 1960–2000

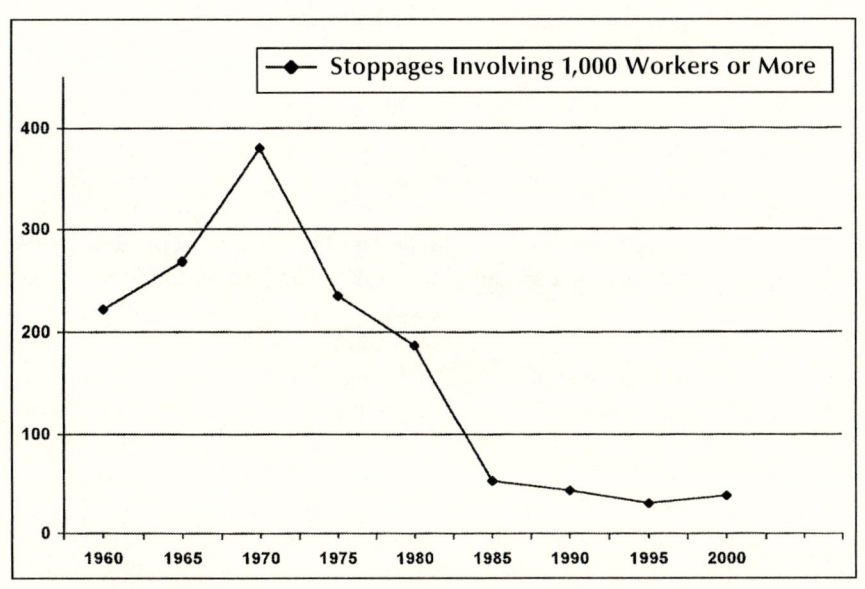

WORK STOPPAGES INVOLVING 1,000 WORKERS OR MORE 1960–2000

Year	Number of Stoppages	Year	Number of Stoppages
1960	222	1985	54
1965	268	1990	44
1970	381	1995	31
1975	235	2000	39
1980	187		

SOURCE: Bureau of Labor Statistics

The number of work stoppages (strikes and lockouts) has fallen sharply since President Reagan fired the Air Traffic controllers in 1981. The term "stoppages" is the term used by the Bureau of Labor statistics because it includes both strikes and lockouts, which thus includes actions whose initiation is the choice of labor or management. It has no relationship to the numbers listed earlier in the chronology, especially around World War II, because in those days all strikes were counted, and many were "wildcat" strikes that may have included only a few workers on the floor for only a few hours.

In this particular study ranging from 1960 through 2000, stoppages peaked in the 1960s and 1970s when many unions had large influxes of "militant" workers representing the culture of the 1960s and early 1970s. But the recession of 1975 eliminated many of the militants due to layoffs. They found themselves high on the list of people to be laid-off, due both to their limited seniority and due to the fact that both the unions themselves and management were glad to be rid of them.

Once President Reagan fired the Air Traffic Controllers in a perfectly legal way (it had been legal for decades, but no one else had enforced it), management in general not only followed his example in similar cases, but began to hire consultants to teach them how to get rid of unions in other ways, all of them quite legal for many years. The unions were slow to react to the new aggressive style of management (which unions had been using for decades, often illegally), but they were able to recognize that the old techniques were no longer going to work. As a result, the number of strikes fell off to all-time lows, even though management began to use the lockout technique more often. This figure applies almost completely to the private sector, because strikes in the public sector are generally illegal. The public sector law is now being enforced, as both the Air Traffic Controllers and those New Jersey teachers who were called in to court in alphabetical order in early 2002 by a judge and sent off to a jail cell for disobeying his order to return to work exemplify. It is apparent that illegal actions by union members will no longer be tolerated.

Appendix 5: Minimum Wage in the United States 1938–2002

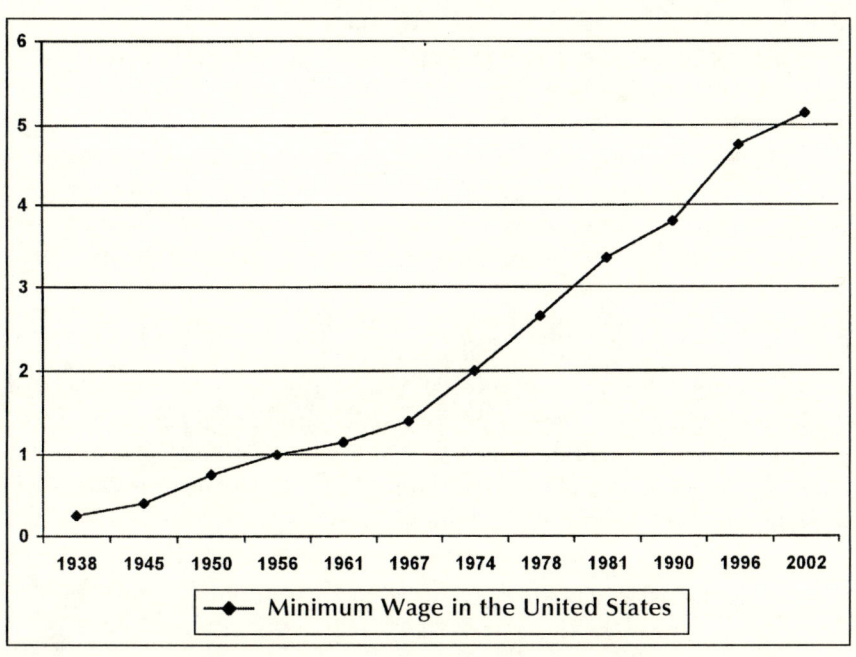

MINIMUM WAGE IN THE UNITED STATES
1938–2002

Year	Wage	Year	Wage
1938	0.25	1974	2.00
1945	0.40	1978	2.65
1950	0.75	1981	3.35
1956	1.00	1990	3.80
1961	1.15	1996	4.75
1967	1.40	2002	5.15

SOURCE: Bureau of Labor Statistics

The first official minimum wage became effective on June 25, 1938, with the enactment of the Fair Labor Standards Act by the Roosevelt Administration. It was one of many items enacted by the government in the 1930s that was meant to benefit all workers, not just union workers, and it is entirely controlled by the federal government. Unions have nothing to do with minimum wage except to urge their representatives in Congress to make it higher more often.

In fact, into the 1900s, Sam Gompers, President of the AFL, continued to oppose having items such as the minimum wage and maximum working hours set by the government. He believed unions could do better on their own via collective bargaining. If the government set a standard, he felt employers would use the minimum wage, for example, more as a ceiling than a floor in bargaining. He also opposed national policies in these areas because they would weaken the tie of workers to their union as their main benefactor.

The administration recognized that if unions were in charge of such things as the minimum wage, only union members would benefit from increases in the wage. This argument was true of many things, and that is why, as described in the Introduction, the 1930s saw the passage of many "employment laws" that operated outside the unions, in addition to "labor laws" that covered private employers and unions.

Any state is free to enact minimum wage laws different from those of the federal government, as long as the state law gives a higher wage. Thus, although the government minimum wage has climbed from 25 cents an hour in 1938, when first enacted, to $5.15 today (an increase of over 20 times), the state of Washington has a minimum wage of $6.90 followed by California and Massachusetts at $6.75 each.

APPENDIX 6: BIOGRAPHIES OF KEY LABOR LEADERS

This appendix lists the six labor leaders in the United States who had the most to do with beginning the organized labor movement and making it grow after the ruling of Judge Shaw in Massachusetts in 1842 that unions were not illegal. The key leaders are listed roughly in order of their appearance in organized labor, brief biographical information, and their key contributions are listed below. They are Samuel Gompers, William Green, George Meany, John L. Lewis, Philip Murray, and Walter Reuther.

Samuel Gompers—Gompers was born in England in 1950, and came to the United States in 1863. He died in 1924 at the age of 74. Gompers is clearly the "father" of organized labor in the United States. He is best known for founding the American Federation of Labor (AFL) in 1886. He earlier helped to found The Federation of Organized Trades and Labor Unions in 1881 as a cautious political move among the groups agitating for a national organization, and by 1883 he had moved up to preside over its convention. None of these early groups were actually unions. They were federations of unions where dues and funds moved back and forth between unions "affiliated" with the central organization, which provided help and information to individual unions as appropriate, and provided a central spokesman for "labor" as a whole.

Gompers cleverly closed his federation after the Haymarket riot in Chicago to escape the negative image all union organizations were being associated with over that affair, and had it reborn as the AFL, of which he was the president. He remained president every year but one from 1886 until he died in 1924. He almost single-handedly promoted the growth of the AFL during some very difficult years for organized labor, and he was President Wilson's main labor advisor before and after World War I. Gompers was famous for saying that what labor wanted was "more," and he religiously avoided having his union used to promote other social goals or to further political goals as the Knights of Labor and Socialists did. That approach left the AFL standing as the number one union federation into the 1920s.

William Green—Green was on of the three famous leaders to come out of the mines (Lewis and Murray are the others). Green was born in 1873 in Ohio, and was the son of an English coal miner who immigrated to the United States. Green became a miner at the age of 16 and worked his way up to become president of the Ohio District in the United Mine Workers when he was 32. After a quick detour into public life as a member of the Ohio Senate, he became secretary-treasurer of the miners' union in 1912 and worked closely with Gompers in the AFL. From that position he was elected President of the AFL when Gompers died in 1924 when he was 51 years old. Green held the job until he died in 1952 at age 79.

Green carried the torch for the AFL through the revolution of the labor laws in the 1930s, holding the federation together when John L. Lewis created the CIO and left the AFL in 1938. He became very frail as he aged through the 1940s, turning over much of the AFL's day-to-day business to George Meany, who was his second in command. Green was not nearly as dynamic and aggressive as the other labor leaders listed here, but he kept the AFL functioning and growing as he followed the teachings of Gompers.

George Meany—Meany was a plumber in a New York union so hard to get into that one literally had to be a family member to get in when times were tight (Meany followed his father). But he was much more interested in the business side of the union, and he became secretary-treasurer of the AFL (one step down from the top) in 1939 when he was only 45. This gave him the edge he needed to become president in 1952. Meany presided over the reunification of the AFL and CIO in 1955, when Walter Reuther was president of the CIO and gladly agreed to have Meany run the combined AFL-CIO. Reuther preferred to run the UAW, and he assumed Meany would retire in due course. But Meany made it clear he would never retire on his own, and he ran the AFL-CIO until December of 1979, stepping down just before his death in January 1980 at age 86. This meant the AFL had only three leaders in its first 94 years: Gompers, Green, and Meany. Meany was violently anti-communist and he pushed hard for the expulsion of communist-led unions from the CIO. He also gave John L. Lewis probably the hardest lecture of his life when he lectured Lewis on the issue of the communists originally brought into the CIO when the 1947 AFL convention was discussing the "loyalty oath" required by the 1947 Taft-Hartley bill. That lecture marked the end of Lewis' career as a top labor leader, and the beginning of Meany's position at the top. Meany made lots of enemies in his "take no prisoners" approach, but no one questioned his word. Meany told it like it was, good or bad, and he had the full respect of Congress. Cause and effect is hard to pinpoint, but labor's sharpest decline began with his death.

John L. Lewis—Lewis was a man of the mines (like Green and Murray). He was born in Iowa in 1880, joined his father in the mines as a teenager, and slowly worked his way up to become President of the United Mine Workers in 1920. As the biggest and most powerful union in the AFL, he constantly challenged Gompers (and later Green) to form industrial (vertical) unions to sign-up the potential union members in the big mass-production companies forming since the 1920s. Lewis became friendly with Roosevelt in the early 1930s, as Roosevelt saw Lewis as the source of large potential blocks of voters while Lewis saw Roosevelt as a patron who would give Lewis the president's ear as his labor advisor.

Lewis formed a Committee for Industrial Organization within the AFL in 1935, and when told to cease and desist, he took his group out of the AFL, renamed it the Congress for Industrial Organization in 1938 (still the CIO), and signed up new union members at a great pace. But he felt betrayed by Roosevelt for losing the adviser position, and bitterly opposed Roosevelt's third term election in 1940, saying he (Lewis) would resign from the CIO if Roosevelt won, taking it as a show of non-confidence by the CIO. Roosevelt won, and Lewis ungraciously quit the CIO, leaving his long-time friend Philip Murray in charge. When Murray refused to be a lap dog for Lewis, Lewis took his miners union out of the CIO in 1942, and used it to embark on a capricious course of strikes that brought down the voters' wrath on labor in 1946, resulting in the Taft-Hartley bill in 1947. After that, no one trusted Lewis, and he was essentially shunned. When the AFL and CIO merged in 1955, Lewis was not invited to attend and his suggestions were ignored. He left the miners' union in 1960 at the age of 80, and died in obscurity in 1969 at the age of 89.

Philip Murray—The last of the coal miners in the pantheon. Murray was born in Scotland in 1886, and joined his father in the mines at the age of 10. The family emigrated to the coalmines near Pittsburgh in 1902. He worked his way up to vice-president of the United Mine Workers in 1920, the year John L. Lewis became president. Murray worked with Lewis for the next 20 years, helping to form the CIO, and took over as president in 1940 when Lewis dramatically quit. Murray was one of the most respected labor leaders of his time. He helped the CIO grow during World War II, earning the complete trust of Roosevelt and Truman, but when it came time to throw out the communist-led unions, it was his great credibility that gave the movement the impetus it needed to do so. Murray died in 1952 at the age of 66.

Walter Reuther—Reuther was born to be a union leader, as his father Valentine was a true socialist and thought unions were the ideal vehicle to bring the whole world to socialism. As a young boy (born in 1907) Reuther joined the after-dinner discussions about socialism. Reuther moved up through the CIO ranks, becoming president of the United Automobile Workers (UAW) in 1946, and later the president of the CIO when Philip Murray died in 1952. But Reuther turned down the number two position in the newly formed AFL-CIO in 1955 because he didn't want anyone over him in his preferred position as president of the UAW.

Reuther was a great union leader and established many new concepts in bargaining, including contracts of more than one year, COLAs, wage increases based on productivity gains, a guaranteed annual wage, etc. But he was obsessed with unions as a vehicle for social change, and he had a desire to be an absolute leader. He faded after the 1955 merger, and when he took the UAW out of the AFL-CIO just before he was killed in a 1979 plane crash, no other unions went with him.

BIBLIOGRAPHY

This bibliography shows the key books consulted in putting together this chronology. I discovered something about these books that needs to be offered as a caveat before they are used for reference purposes.

First, it appears that nearly anyone who undertakes to write a general or specific history about unions has a built-in bias in favor of them. These biases are freely admitted in nearly all cases, and they generally take the form of a statement in the Preface or Introduction of the book saying that the author(s) sincerely believe that the United States is much better off, or would be much better off, with strong unions butting heads with management. The academic books treat this bias in a professional way. Some other authors have seen the unions as struggling under the heel of "management," using a code word for what in Europe has sometimes been called fascists.

Any reader of a book such as this one will easily be able to discern such a bias in the books in the bibliography, especially since there is no effort to hide it. The important point to be made is that it often will be necessary to refer to a number of books to get somewhere near the truth of what happened in a given conflict.

The famous bloody strikes in history usually follow the same plot. Replacement workers arrive to take jobs left by strikers, and various federal or state troops or agencies such as the Pinkertons are brought in to protect them. The strikers fight back with bullets, and fatal results, and the "who shot John" and "who shot first" discussions begin. In the most biased books, union members always wear the white hats, and in defense of their heroes the authors are capable of such phrases as a "peaceful armed mob" to describe union men marching to battle. But each book adds some useful information and if one struggles through them all, one will approach closer to the truth.

A second point is that the most recently published books discuss the "decline" of labor as something that has already happened, and their theme is either to record for posterity how it happened or to attempt to assist in bringing labor back. There is no way to escape their conclusions that the struggle has already been or soon will be lost. This is a conclusion I reached on my own after poring through the books listed in the bibliography and elsewhere. It was something of a shock; I originally had no such idea.

The most seemingly objective books covering the labor movement since the country began, and which are quite academic in style, are *Organized Labor in American History* by Philip Taft, and *American Labor* by Henry Pelling. But these books were published in 1964 and 1960 respectively, so they do not tell the rest of the story. Two of the biographies are quite objective, allowing for the fact they are biographies. These are *Samuel Gompers and Organized Labor in America* by Harold C. Lindsay, and *Walter Reuther and the Rise of the Auto Workers* by John Barnard. But both books end with the death of their subjects, in 1924 and 1970 respectively.

I have mixed feelings about *An Injury to All: The Decline of American Unionism* by Kim Moody, which covers roughly the period from Truman to Reagan. The book was published in 1988, and thus misses the last decade of the century, while starting at what could be the peak period for unions. Moody was a staff member of the Detroit-based publication *Labor Notes*, and was a highly respected labor journalist in North America when he wrote the book. He admits to a Marxist leaning, but his writing could be said to be biased only in the way a sports journalist would be while writing about the history of his favorite team. He is extremely professional and deeply knowledgeable about his subject. His title is taken from the labor slogan of the 1880s; "an injury to one is an injury to all." More in sadness than anger, Moody carefully chronicles the fall of labor from its high to its low (at the end of the 1980s), but he makes it clear he sees no turnaround for labor unless "working class" unionism can replace a failing "business unionism" (maybe in other countries if not here). My feeling is he was saying all the proper words about possible future turnarounds without much conviction that it can happen.

Probably the single most objective book is *Rekindling the Movement: Labor's Quest for Relevance in the 21st Century* by Lowell Turner et al. This book is a collection of articles and essays mainly by academics, who are writing on the theme that we all must admit organized labor has experienced a great decline and there are both successes and failures to learn from. The only bias is in favor of an economy in which unions are involved to provide a degree of balance, but the tone of the book is a feeling of sadness that it's all over. The last line of the book is a summing up: "While wishing the American labor movement well, because of the difficult nature of the task at hand, I can only predict that union revitalization will be an extremely difficult uphill struggle."

Banner, Lois W. *Elizabeth Cady Stanton, A Radical for Women's Rights*. 2nd ed. Boston: Little, Brown, 1980.

_____. *Women in Modern America: A Brief History*. New York: Harcourt Brace Jovanovich, 1984.

Barnard, John. *Walter Reuther and the Rise of the Auto Workers*. Boston: Little, Brown, 1983.

Bernstein, Irving. *A Caring Society*. Boston: Houghton Mifflin, 1985.

_____. *The Lean Years*. Baltimore: Penguin Books, 1960.

Bird, Stewart; Dan Georgakas, and Deborah Shaffer. *Solidarity Forever*. Chicago: Lake View Press, 1985.

Brecher, Jeremy. *Strike!* Cambridge, Mass.: South End Press, 1997.

Bridgwater, William, and Seymour Kurtz, eds., *The Columbia Encyclopedia*. New York: Columbia University Press, 1963.

Dubofsky, Melvin. *We Shall Be All*. New York: Quadrangle/The New York Times Book Co., 1969.

Gold, Michael Evan. *An Introduction to Labor Law*. Ithaca, N.Y.: IRL/Cornell Paperbacks, 1998.

Lichtenstein, Nelson. *Walter Reuther: The Most Dangerous Man in Detroit*. Chicago: University of Illinois Press, 1995.

Livesay, Harold C. *Samuel Gompers and Organized Labor in America*. Prospect Heights, Ill.: Waveland Press, 1993.

Mailhot, Ernie; Judy Stranahan, and Jack Barnes. *The Eastern Airlines Strike*. New York: Pathfinder, 1991.

McGeveran, William A., Jr., Editorial Director. *The World Almanac and Book of Facts*. New York: World Almanac Education Group, 2002.

Miester, Dick, and Anne Loftis. *A Long Time Coming*. New York: Macmillan, 1977.

Mishel, Lawrence; Jared Bernstein, and John Schmitt. *The State of Working America, 2000/2001*. Ithaca, N.Y.: Cornell University Press, 2001.

Moody, Kim. *An Injury to All: The Decline of American Unionism*. New York: Verso, 1988.

Murray, R. Emmett. *The Lexicon of Labor*. New York: The New Press, 1998.

Pelling, Henry. *American Labor*. Chicago: University of Chicago Press, 1960.

Puette, William J. *Through Jaundiced Eyes*. Ithaca, N.Y.: IRL Press, 1992.

Rachleff, Peter. *Hard-Pressed in the Heartland*. Boston: South End Press, 1993.

Robinson, Archie. *George Meany and His Times*. New York: Simon and Schuster, 1981.

Taft, Philip. *Organized Labor in American History*. New York: Harper & Row, 1964.

Turner, Lowell; Harry C. Katz, and Richard W. Hurd, eds., *Rekindling the Movement: Labor's Quest for Relevance in the 21st Century*. Ithaca, N.Y.: Cornell University Press, 2001.

INDEX

Aaron, Hank 12/27/2001
Adande, J. A. 12/27/2001
AFL (American Federation of Labor) 7/29/1863, 12/8/1886, 1/1/1887, 12/5/1888, 7/6/1892, 5/10/1894, 7/4/1897, 9/10/1897, 12/31/1902, 1/2/1905, 3/18/1908, 12/23/1908, 10/1/1910, 1/11/1912, 4/6/1917, 9/17/1917, 4/1/1922, 12/13/1924, 3/23/1932, 5/17/1933, 11/9/1935, 11/23/1935, 9/5/1936, 11/14/1938, 9/1/1939, 10/25/1940, 1/22/1942, 5/25/1942, 9/11/1946, 12/12/1947, 11/5/1949, 5/23/1950, 11/9/1952, 11/25/1952, 4/7/1953, 2/8/1955, 12/5/1955, 1/14/1980
AFL-CIO 2/8/1955, 12/5/1955, 9/14/1959, 7/1/1968, 11/7/1972, 11/2/1976, 1/14/1980, 1/18/1991, 10/31/1995, 1/1/1996, 12/6/2001, 2/2/2002, 2/7/2002
Agricultural Labor Relations Board 1/24/2002
Alabama 12/5/1888, 5/9/1970
Alliance for Labor Action (ALA) 7/1/1968, 11/7/1972
Amalgamated Steel Workers 7/6/1892
Amalgamated Labor Union of Terre Haute 8/2/1881
American Airlines 2/2/2002
American Anti-Boycott Association 12/23/1908
American Bridge Company 10/1/1910
American Labor Union 1/2/1905, 6/27/1905
American Miners Union 7/28/1861

American Railway Union 6/30/1893, 5/10/1894
American Woolen Company 1/11/1912
anthracite 4/6/1868, 4/14/1874, 12/5/1888, 9/10/1897, 9/17/1900
Arsenal of Democracy 9/1/1939
Association of Flight Attendants 2/1/2002
Atlantic City, NJ 11/9/1935
atomic bomb 9/17/1945
Austin, MN 7/15/1987

Babbitt, George (Governor) 10/31/1995
Baltimore 12/2/1850, 8/20/1866
Baltimore and Ohio Railroad Strike 7/6/1877
Barry, T. B. 5/1/1886
Baseball Hall of Fame 12/27/2001
baseball players' union 12/27/2001
battle of the overpass 5/23/1950
Beck, Dave 9/14/1959
"behead the redhead" 7/1/1968
Belmont, August 9/17/1900
Berkman, Alexander 7/6/1892
Berlin 10/25/1940
bituminous 12/5/1888, 7/4/1897, 9/17/1900, 5/1/1943
Black Lake Resort Area 7/1/1968, 5/9/1970
Borman, Frank 1/18/1991
Boston 12/2/1850
Breena, John 1/11/1912
Brewery Workers 12/31/1902
Brotherhood of Locomotive Engineers 5/8/1983
Brotherhood of Railroad Firemen 6/30/1893

131

Index

Buck's Range and Stove Company 12/23/1908
Bush, President George W. 3/5/2002

California 10/1/1910, 1/1/2002, 1/24/2002, 2/7/2002
California Angels 12/27/2001
California State Federation of Labor 10/1/1910
Campbell, Alex 4/14/1874
Carnegie, Andrew 7/6/1892, 9/17/1900
Carpenter's Union 11/14/1938
Carter, President Jimmy 11/2/1976, 11/4/1980
Caterpillar Strike 1/1/1996
Catholic Church vs. Knights of Labor 1/1/1878
Chavez-Thompson, Linda 10/31/1995
Chemical Workers 11/14/1938
Chicago 7/6/1877, 5/1/1886, 6/30/1893, 5/10/1894, 1/2/1905, 10/1/1910, 9/17/1917
Child Labor Law 10/15/1914
China 2/23/2002
Chrysler 11/21/1945, 5/9/1970, 10/3/2001
Cigar Makers Union 7/29/1863, 5/13/1886
CIO (Committee/Congress for Industrial Organizations) 12/8/1886, 11/9/1935, 11/23/1935, 9/5/1936, 11/14/1938, 9/1/1939, 10/25/1940, 1/22/1942, 5/25/1942, 9/17/1945, 1/21/1945, 9/11/1946, 12/12/1947, 11/5/1949, 11/9/1952, 4/7/1953, 2/8/1955, 12/5/1955, 1/14/1980
Citizens Crusade Against Poverty 7/1/1968
Citizens Industrial Association 12/23/1908
Civil War 1/1/1863, 2/13/1865, 4/23/1869
class war prisoner 9/17/1917
Clayton Act 10/15/1914, 4/6/1917
"clear it with Sidney" 10/25/1940
Cleveland, President Grover 5/1/1886, 5/10/1894
codes of fair practice 5/17/1933
Coeur d'Alene, ID 1/2/1905
COLA (Cost of Living Adjustment) 5/23/1950
Combined War Labor Board, Combined Labor War Board, Combined Labor Victory Committee, War Labor Board 1/22/1942
Communist (Party and people) 11/14/1938, 10/25/1940, 5/25/1942, 12/12/1947, 11/5/1949, 5/23/1950, 11/7/1972
Congress 4/6/1868, 3/18/1908, 5/17/1933, 5/1/1943, 5/17/1946, 11/7/1972, 8/5/1981; 1946 election 11/5/1946

Continental Airlines 2/2/2002
Continental Congress 6/27/1905
Creighton, John 12/5/2001
Cripple Creek, CO 1/2/1905

Danbury Hatter's Case 3/18/1908, 12/23/1908
Darrow, Clarence 10/1/1910
Davis, David (Judge) 8/20/1866
Dawkins, Richard 12/27/2001
Debs, Eugene V. 7/5/1859, 6/30/1893, 5/10/1894, 7/4/1897, 12/31/1902, 1/2/1905, 6/27/1905
Decatur, IL 10/31/1995, 1/1/1996
deLeon, Daniel 6/27/1905
Delta Airlines 2/1/2002
Denver, CO 5/10/1894, 1/2/1905
Department of Industrial Relations 1/24/2002
Department of Justice 5/10/1894
Detroit 5/23/1950, 7/1/1968, 9/17/1986
DiMaggio, Joe 12/27/2001
Dirksen, Everett 11/22/1963
Dodge Revolutionary Union Movement (DRUM) 7/1/1968
Donahue, Tom 10/31/1995
Doyle, Michael 4/14/1874
Drew, Walter 10/1/1910
dual unionism 5/13/1886, 1/2/1905, 2/8/1955

Eastern Airlines bankruptcy 1/18/1991, 9/11/2001, 12/5/2001, 2/14/2002
Economic Development Department 1/24/2002
eight-hour day 5/1/1886, 9/17/1900
Eisenhower, President Dwight D. 9/14/1959, 11/4/1980
Elizabeth, PA 4/6/1868
Emancipation Proclamation 1/1/1863
Erectors Association 10/1/1910
Ettor, Joe 1/11/1912

Fair Employment and Housing Departments 1/24/2002
Federation of Organized Trades and Labor Unions, the 8/2/1881, 5/13/1886, 12/8/1886
Fitzsimmons, Frank 7/1/1968
Flynn, Elizabeth Gurley 9/17/1917
Ford 11/21/1945, 10/3/2001
Ford, President Gerald 11/2/1976
Ford Foundation 7/1/1968
Frick, H. C. 7/6/1892

General Managers Association 5/10/1894
General Motors 11/21/1945, 5/23/1950, 9/17/1986, 10/3/2001

Gerald, Leo W. 12/4/2001
Germany 9/1/1939, 12/5/1955, 10/3/2001
Giovanitti, Arturo 1/11/1912
Golden, John 1/11/1912
Gompers, Henry 1/1/1887
Gompers, Samuel 7/29/1863, 8/2/1881,
   5/1/1886, 5/13/1886, 12/8/1886, 1/1/1887,
   12/5/1888, 7/2/1890, 7/6/1892,
   5/10/1894 , 7/4/1897, 9/17/1900,
   12/31/1902, 1/2/1905, 3/18/1908,
   12/23/1908, 1/11/1912, 4/6/1917,
   9/17/1917, 4/1/1922, 12/13/1924,
   1/22/1942, 11/9/1952, 12/5/1955,
   5/9/1970, 1/14/1980, 2/2/2002
Gompers, Solomon 7/29/1863
Gowen, Franklin 4/14/1874
Great Northern Railroad 6/30/1893
Great Society program 11/22/1963
Green, William 12/13/1924, 3/23/1932,
   5/17/1933, 11/23/1935, 9/5/1936,
   11/14/1938, 10/25/1940, 1/22/1942,
   12/12/1947, 11/9/1952, 11/25/1952,
   5/9/1970, 1/14/1980
Greenback Labor Party 1/1/1878
Griffith, Robert 9/14/1959
guaranteed annual wage 5/23/1950

Haggerty, Father Thomas J. 6/27/1905
Hanna, Mark 9/17/1900
Hatter's Union 3/18/1908
Hayes, President Rutherford B. 7/6/1877
Haymarket Square Riot 5/1/1886,
   5/13/1886, 12/8/1886, 10/1/1910
Hays, Frank 4/1/1922
Haywood, Alan S. 11/25/1952
Haywood, William D. "Big Bill" 1/2/1905,
   6/27/1905, 1/11/1912, 9/17/1917
Hazelton, PA 9/10/1897
Herrin (IL) Massacre 7/4/1897, 4/1/1922
Hiberians, Ancient Order of 4/14/1874
Hill (Hillstrom), Joe 9/17/1917
Hillman, Sidney 10/25/1940
Hitler, Adolf 3/4/1933, 9/1/1939,
   10/25/1940, 5/25/1942
Hoffa, Jimmy 7/1/1968
Homestead Strike 7/6/1892, 9/17/1900
Hoover, President Herbert 3/23/1932
Hormel Strike 7/15/1987
Howard, Pullman Vice President
   5/10/1894
Humphrey, Hubert 11/7/1972
Hutcheson, Bill 11/14/1938

Ickes, Harold 5/1/1943
Idaho 1/2/1905, 9/17/1917
Illinois 8/20/1866, 12/28/1869, 5/10/1894,
   7/4/1987

Indiana 12/28/1869, 7/6/1877, 10/1/1910
Indianapolis, IN 5/10/1894
Industrial Workers of the World (IWW)
   12/31/1902, 6/27/1905, 1/11/1912,
   4/6/1917, 9/17/1917
injunctions 3/23/1932
International Harvester Corporation
   5/1/1886
Iran 11/2/1976
Iron and Steelworkers 2/13/1865
Iron Molders 7/5/1859, 8/20/1866
Iron Workers Union 10/1/1910
ITU (International Typographical Union)
   12/2/1850, 8/2/1881

Japan 9/17/1945, 12/5/1955, 5/9/1970,
   9/17/1986, 10/3/2001
Jarrett, John 8/2/1881
John Deere Corporation 1/1/1996
Johnson, Hiram (Governor) 10/1/1910
Johnson, President Lyndon B. (and
   administration) 6/23/1947, 11/22/1963,
   7/1/1968
Jones, John P. 4/14/1874
Judge fines UMW and Lewis for contempt
   9/11/1946

Kelley, Edward 4/14/1874
Kennedy, President John F. (and adminis-
   tration) 6/23/1947, 9/14/1959,
   11/22/1963
Kennedy, Robert 11/22/1963
Kent State 5/9/1970
Kerrigan, James 4/14/1874
King, Martin Luther, Jr. 7/1/1968
King Coal 12/31/1902
Kirkland, Lane 11/25/1952, 11/2/1976,
   10/31/1995
Knights of Labor 12/28/1869, 1/1/1878,
   8/2/1881, 5/1/1886, 5/13/1886,
   12/8/1886, 12/5/1888, 7/4/1897,
   12/31/1902, 1/2/1905
Knights of St. Crispin 4/23/1869
Kremlin Wall 9/17/1917

Labor Day 5/1/1886
La Guardia, Fiorello H. 3/23/1932,
   3/4/1933
Landrum, Phil 9/14/1959
Landrum-Griffith Act (Labor-Management
   Reporting and Disclosure Act)
   6/23/1947, 9/14/1959, 11/22/1963,
   8/5/1981
Laredo, TX 12/13/1924
Las Vegas 12/6/2001
Lattimer (PA) Massacre 9/10/1897
Law, Michael 4/14/1874

Index

Lawrence, MA 1/11/1912
Lawrence (MA) Textile Mills Strike 1/11/1912
Leadville, CO 1/2/1905
Leavenworth 9/17/1917
legacy cost 12/4/2001
Lehigh, PA 9/17/1900
Lester, William J. 9/17/1917
Lewis, John L. 7/28/1861, 12/5/1888, 4/1/1922, 12/13/1924, 5/17/1933, 11/9/1935, 11/23/1935, 9/5/1936, 11/14/1938, 9/1/1939, 10/25/1940, 1/22/1942, 5/25/1942, 5/1/1943, 9/17/1945, 11/21/1945, 9/11/1946, 11/5/1946, 12/12/1947, 5/23/1950, 11/9/1952, 12/5/1955, 5/9/1970, 1/14/1980, 1/23/2002
Lewis, Kathryn 12/12/1947
Lewisburg Federal Prison 7/1/1968
little steel formula 5/1/1943
Loewe and Company 3/18/1908
Loewe Boycott 3/18/1908
LoPezzi, Anna 1/11/1912
Lorenzo, Frank 1/18/1991
Los Angeles Times 10/1/1910, 10/3/2001, 12/5/2001, 12/27/2001, 2/23/2002
Ludlow, CO 9/10/1897

Machinists Union (International Association of Machinists) 8/5/1981
Madden, Judge J. Warren 7/27/1935
maintenance of membership 5/1/1943
Massachusetts 1/1/2002
Master Workmen 12/28/1869
Mauchunk, PA 4/14/1874
May Day 5/1/1886
Mays, Willie 12/27/2001
McBride, John 5/101/894
McClelland, John L. (Senator) 9/14/1959, 11/22/1963
McDonald, David J. 11/25/1952
McKay Stitcher 4/23/1869
McManigal, Ortie 10/1/1910
McNamara, James 10/1/1910
McNamara, John J. 10/1/1910
McParland, James 4/14/1874
Meany, George 1/22/1942, 5/25/1942, 6/23/1947, 12/12/1947, 11/9/1952, 11/25/1952, 2/8/1955, 12/5/1955, 9/14/1959, 7/1/1968, 5/9/1970, 11/7/1972, 11/2/1976, 1/14/1980, 10/31/1995
Metalliferous Miners 1/2/1905
Mexico 12/13/1924
Mexico City 12/13/1924
Miami 2/8/1955
Miami Beach 7/1/1968

Milwaukee, WI 4/23/1869
minimum wage 1/1/2002
Mitchell, John 9/17/1900, 12/31/1902, 12/23/1908
Molly Maguires 4/6/1868, 12/28/1869, 4/14/1874, 5/1/1886, 9/10/1897
Monongahlea River 7/6/1892
Morgan, J.P. 9/17/1900
Moscow 9/17/1917, 10/25/1940, 5/25/1942
Moyer, Charles H. 1/2/1905, 6/27/1905
Munley, Thomas 4/14/1874
Murray, Philip 10/25/1940, 1/22/1942, 5/25/1942, 12/12/1947, 11/5/1949, 5/23/1950, 11/9/1952, 5/9/1970, 1/14/1980
Musial, Stan 12/27/2001

Nader, Ralph 7/1/1968
National Association of Manufacturers (NAM) 7/4/1897, 12/23/1908
National Civic Foundation (NCF) 9/17/1900
National Council of Defense 4/6/1917
National Council of Industrial Defense 12/23/1908
National Defense Advisory Commission 10/25/1940
National Industrial Recovery Act (NIRA) 5/17/1933, 5/27/1935, 7/27/1935
National Labor Board 8/5/1933
National Labor Relations Board (NLRB) 8/5/1933, 9/1/1939, 12/12/1947, 7/15/1987, 1/1/1996
National Labor Union 8/20/1866
National Mediation Board 2/1/2002
National Progressive Union of Miners zand Mine Laborers, the 12/5/1888
Navy operated refineries 9/17/1945
new voice group 10/31/1995
New York 12/2/1850, 7/29/1863, 7/6/1877, 7/6/1892, 2/8/1955, 11/7/1972, 7/15/1987, 9/11/2001
New York Mets 12/27/2001
Nissan no-vote for UAW 10/3/2001
Nixon, President Richard M. 9/14/1959, 11/7/1972, 11/2/1976
Norris, George W. (Senator) 3/23/1932
Norris-LaGuardia Act 3/23/1932
no-strike pledge (World War II) 5/1/1943
November 1946 vote 9/17/1945

Ohio 12/28/1869, 7/6/1877
Oil Workers International Union 9/17/1945
OSHA 2/23/2002
overfull employment 3/4/1933

Index

P9 Union of UFCW 7/15/1987
Pana, IL 7/4/1897
pardon for Nixon 11/2/1976
pardons for IWW 9/17/1917
PATCO (Professional Air Traffic Controllers Organization) Strike 8/5/1981, 10/31/1995
Pearl Harbor 3/4/1933, 1/22/1942
Pennsylvania 4/6/1868, 12/28/1869, 7/6/1877, 12/5/1888
pension benefits 5/23/1950
Phelps Dodge Strike 10/31/1995
Philadelphia 12/2/1850, 7/5/1859, 4/6/1868, 12/28/1869
Pinkerton, Alan 4/14/1874
Pinkerton Detective Agency (the Pinkertons) 4/14/1874, 5/1/1886, 7/6/1892
Pittsburgh, PA 8/2/1881, 7/6/1892, 7/4/1897
Poland 9/1/1939, 10/25/1940
Populist Party 12/31/1902
Port Carbon, PA 4/6/1868, 4/14/1874
postal workers' 1970 strike 8/5/1981
Pottsville, PA 4/14/1874
Powderley, Terence V. 1/1/1878, 8/2/1881, 5/1/1886, 5/13/1886
Protest Conference 3/18/1908
public sector unions 12/6/2001
Pullman, George M. 5/10/1894
Pullman, Town of 5/10/1894
Pullman Strike 6/30/1893, 5/10/1894, 12/31/1902, 3/18/1908
"put Walter in a halter" 7/1/1968

quicken the work pace 9/17/1986

reader for cigar rolling 7/29/1863
Reagan, President Ronald 11/2/1976, 11/4/1980, 8/5/1981, 9/17/1986
Rehnquist, William 9/17/1986
Reuther, May 5/9/1970
Reuther, Valentine 5/23/1950
Reuther, Victor 9/17/1986
Reuther, Walter 9/1/1939, 10/25/1940, 1/22/1942, 11/21/1945, 5/23/1950, 11/25/1952, 12/5/1955, 7/1/1968, 5/9/1970, 1/14/1980, 9/17/1986
Rockefeller, John D. 7/2/1890
Rodgers, Ray 7/15/1987
Roosevelt, Eleanor 5/23/1950
Roosevelt, President Franklin D. 1/1/1887, 3/4/1933, 5/17/1933, 8/5/1933, 11/14/1938, 9/1/1939, 10/25/1940, 1/22/1942, 5/25/1942, 5/1/1943, 11/5/1946, 5/23/1950, 11/9/1952, 11/22/1963
Roosevelt, President Theodore 9/17/1900, 4/6/1917

Royal Family, the (Reuther) 5/23/1950
Rubber Workers 11/14/1938
Russia 1/11/1912, 10/25/1940, 5/25/1942, 5/23/1950
Ruth, Babe 5/25/1942

sabotage 6/27/1905, 7/1/1968
St. Louis 7/6/1877, 12/23/1908
St. Matthew's Cathedral 1/14/1980
Salt Lake City, UT 9/17/1917
Saturn automobile 9/17/1986
Scalia, Antonin 9/17/1986
Schnitzler, Bill 12/5/1955
Schuylkill, PA 4/6/1868, 9/17/1900
Section 7(a) 5/17/1933
Service International Employees Union (SIEU) 10/31/1995
Sherman, C.O. (IWW President) 6/27/1905
Sherman, John (Senator) 7/2/1890
Sherman Antitrust Act 7/2/1890, 5/10/1894, 12/31/1902, 3/18/1908, 10/15/1914
Shinall, Jim 1/1/1996
Siney, John 4/6/1868
sit-down strike 9/1/1939
Slave Labor Act 6/23/1947
sliding scale 2/13/1865, 4/6/1868
Smith-Connally Bill (War Labor Disputes Act) 5/1/1943
Smyrna, TN 10/3/2001
Social Democratic Ticket 1/2/1905
Socialist (Party and persons) 7/5/1859, 8/2/1881, 5/13/1886, 12/8/1886, 1/1/1887, 6/30/1893, 5/10/1894, 1/2/1905, 6/27/1905, 1/11/1912
Sons of Vulcan 7/6/1892
Soviet Union 9/17/1917
Springhill, TN 9/17/1986
Staley Company Strike 1/1/1996
steamer, "Little Bill" 7/6/1892
Steunberg, Frank (Governor) 1/2/1905
Stevens, Uriah 12/28/1869, 1/1/1878
Strikes of 1877 7/6/1877
Supplemental Unemployment Benefit (SUB) 12/5/1955
Supreme Court 5/101/1894, 3/18/1908, 12/23/1908, 10/15/1914, 5/27/1935, 7/27/1935, 9/1/1939
Sweeny, John 10/31/1995, 12/6/2001, 2/2/2002
Sylvis, William H. 7/5/1859, 8/20/1866

Taft, Bob 6/23/1947
Taft-Hartley Act 10/25/1940, 5/25/1942, 5/1/1943, 9/11/1946, enacted 6/23/1947, 12/12/1947, 11/5/1949, 9/14/1959, 11/22/1963, 8/5/1981, 12/27/2001

Index

tax loopholes 8/5/1981
Teamsters 11/14/1938, 7/1/1968, 11/7/1972
Tennessee 5/9/1970
Terre Haute, IN 8/2/1881
Texas Air Corporation 1/18/1991
Tobin, Bill 11/25/1952
Trautman, W.E. (IWW Secretary-Treasurer) 6/27/1905
Treaty of Detroit 5/23/1950
Truman, President Harry S 9/17/1945, 11/21/1945, 5/17/1946, 9/11/1946, 6/23/1947, 5/23/1950, 11/9/1952, 11/2/1976
Truman takes over the railroads 5/17/1946
Trumpka, Richard 10/31/1995

union stock sharing plan 5/23/1950
United Airlines 9/11/2001, 12/5/2001, 2/2/2002, 2/14/2002, 3/6/2002
United Automobile Workers (UAW) 11/14/1938, 9/1/1939, 11/21/1945, 5/23/1950, 12/5/1955, 7/1/1968, 5/9/1970, 11/7/1972, 1/1/1996, 10/3/2001
United Food and Commercial Workers (UFCW) and Trusteeship 7/15/1987
United Mine Workers Journal 5/25/1942, 9/11/1946
United Mine Workers of America (UMW) 12/5/1888, 5/10/1984, 7/4/1897, 9/10/1897, 9/17/1900, 12/31/1902, 4/1/1922, 12/13/1924, 9/1/1939, 10/25/1940, 5/25/1942, 5/1/1943, 9/11/1946, 12/12/1947
United Miners Union 12/5/1888, 11/23/1935
United States Postal Service 5/10/1894
United Textile Workers 1/11/1912
UPS Strike 12/6/2001
US Airways 2/2/2002
U.S. Steel 3/5/2002
U.S. Steel proposed merger 12/4/2001

vanCleve, James 12/23/1908
Vandeveer, George 9/17/1917
Vatican 1/1/1878

Vaughn, Mo 12/27/2001
Verden, IL 7/4/1897
Vietnam 6/23/1947, 11/22/1963, 7/1/1968, 11/7/1972

wages vs. productivity 5/23/1950
Wagner, Robert (Senator) 8/5/1933, 5/27/1935
Wagner Act (National Labor Relations Act) 5/27/1935, 7/27/1935, 11/9/1935, 9/5/1936, 9/1/1939, 5/1/1943, 11/5/1946, 6/23/1947, 12/12/1947, 9/14/1959, 11/22/1963, 8/5/1981
Wallace, George 11/7/1972
Wallace, Henry 11/5/1949
Washington (state) 1/1/2002
Washington, D.C. 11/9/1935, 2/8/1955, 1/14/1980
Washington Post 8/5/1981
Watergate 11/7/1972, 11/2/1976
We Don't Patronize list 12/23/1908
West Virginia 12/28/1869, 12/5/1888, 7/4/1897
Western Conference of Miners 1/2/1905
Western Federation of Miners 1/2/1905, 6/27/1905
Western Labor Union 1/2/1905
Wicks, Pullman Vice President 5/10/1894
wildcat strikes 9/17/1945, 8/5/1981
Williams, Ted 12/27/2001
Wilson, Charles E. 5/23/1950, 12/5/1955
Wilson, President Woodrow 10/15/1914, 4/6/1917, 9/17/1917
Wobblies 9/17/1917
Worcester, MA 4/23/1869
Workforce Investment Board 1/24/2002
Workingmens Benevolent Association 4/6/1868
World Trade Center towers destruction 9/11/2001, 2/2/2002
World War I 12/31/1902, 6/27/1905, 1/11/1912, 4/6/1917, 1/22/1942
World War II 1/1/1863, 9/1/1939, 10/25/1940, 5/25/1942, 11/5/1946, 8/5/1981; strikes 9/17/1945